T0146559

Praise for *#Loneliness: The Virus of the Modern Age*

Throughout history, when the world experiences a great crisis, some unknown with the formula for dissolving that crisis has always arisen. The hand of destiny selects people of troubled and ordinary status and gives them great jobs to do in life as an inspiration and an object lesson to others.

We are facing the biggest problems in human existence in meeting the challenges over the next two decades that hardly any human can escape.

Tony's story of survival through the most difficult childhood and testing times on the streets of London and in the corporate world gave rise to the man who now shares his story and guides us with his intrinsic philosophies. This is only the beginning of what the world will know of this inspiring, selfless being.

His words are beautifully and intelligently crafted into every line and are able to pierce the cocooned world that blocks us from the truth as we permit the noise of our daily reality to control and direct our lives, reprogram our conditioned consciousness, and open our hearts and minds to awaken our genius.

There is no single review that will express the feeling you get when you turn the pages of an essential life manual. I hope my contribution helps you gain an understanding of the magnitude of importance in this message.

Tony has life's gift of transmuting what we all know within us into words that everyone can relate to. This is a most powerful talent.

#Loneliness: The Virus of the Modern Age answers our true calling to reach the next level and starts a revolution in thinking and education and start the journey as the collective oneness we know we are. This is a journey we must all engage in to create heaven on earth and save us from oblivion.

Thank you, Tony, for being the light that others can walk toward, for being the bridge from the shadows to the sunlight, from not knowing to knowing, and thank you for your commitment to the most important contribution to the progression of humanity and the planet.

—Joel Alexander Van der Molen, managing director, Vandercom

Tony explains beautifully the meaning and consequence of loneliness, a universally experienced, major fact of modern life. This book effortlessly points out that we have missed the point and value of connectedness and how without connectedness and love, loneliness can be a killer.

This is a must-read book for everyone to better understand times when we have all been lonely, currently may be lonely, or may experience loneliness in the future. This book breaks the myths about what loneliness is, and if we read it, we will transmute the sea of loneliness into an ocean of oneness.

—Vicki Wusche, author of *Property for the Next Generation*

Thousands upon thousands of books adorn endless bookshelves in bookshops all over the world, and so do millions of pages on the Internet. How on earth is one to know which one will be worth reading?

#Loneliness: The Virus of The Modern Age is a rare book that has something for everyone. No matter how much a hardened critic, how skeptical, how vulnerable, how soft-centered, or how hard-core scientific you may be, rest assured there is something for you in this book.

When the words written are born of hard-earned, sometimes excruciating experiences, crafted in response to the raw imperative to communicate, and driven relentlessly by the unstoppable impulse to nourish, enliven, and heal those in pain who are searching, yearning, even dying for connection and meaning, there is a vitality and energy that transcends the words and touches the soul.

There may be only one line, or it may be the whole book; whatever the case, it will be as if it had been written for you. The fundamental truth about all human experience is that separation and loneliness exist so we might find our way to that place of connection and meaning that resides eternally within.

Tony knows this. He learned it the only way it can be learned—he lived the journey of awakening and surrendering to the experience of isolation and dying to be reborn, heal, and bring that healing to others.

It is a privilege to share his work with you. If you are serious about transformation and change, the exercises are tried and tested and will serve you for a lifetime. Do yourself a favor and read at least the beginning; this man's life and journey are awe-inspiring.

—Dr. Kim A. Jobst, MA, DM, MRCP, MFHom

"Don't be ashamed of your story; it will inspire others" (unknown author). It does indeed. In this emotional yet healing book, Tony relates the most gripping stories that led him home and offered the gifts that he shares with us—the gift of healing wounds and the courage to allow ourselves to embrace our "whol-i-ness." Give yourself this priceless gift that this book is, read it with childlike curiosity, and learn to speak your truth, honor your soul, and center your being. Keep shining and sharing your gifts.

—Mouna Salih

My realization has been that it's the person who writes the book to whom I pay my respects and send salutations. If a wealthy stranger gives you a trunk of gold, whom do you thank? The gold? No! The person who gave you the gold.

I wholeheartedly thank Tony for bringing these astounding insights and knowledge to the world; they bleed out of every chapter; these are jewels of wisdom and information that we would need a lifetime to discover on our own; he reveals with every word a new beginning.

In every chapter, he remarkably unveils the amazing secrets and methods of how to live life in joy and purpose without fear of loneliness and certainly with the absence of loneliness.

As you read each line, you will feel the presence of someone who is truly in sync with your pain, past, future, and dreams; in such a magical way you will experience him holding your hand and bringing a welcome change to your life with subtlety and care.

Tony, through his descriptive and true-life experiences, suspends you in the very room you are reading his book and gives you a three-dimensional view of what pain and loneliness mean.

I have always called Tony the See-Through Coach. By reading this book, he has allowed me to access the deepest part in me; his depth of experience sees through my next step in life. This is refreshing and enlightening, and it's beautifully written.

Thank you, Tony, for seeing through me, for helping my son and my family, and for allowing me to echo your profound message to this world through my work.

Now is the time to wake up! This book will do just that for you.

—Anthony Wade, voice transformational coach, aka Dr. Voice

Tony is a phenomenal speaker and writer with the ability to touch your soul because he speaks from his heart. His style is engaging, engrossing, and profound. He takes his readers through his own heart-wrenching journey that allow them to be reassured that finding peace and healing aloneness is possible in anyone's life journey.

Tony's book is a masterful blend of his personal story and practical exercises that will increase the love, appreciation and joy in your life. This is a life-changing book written by a truly inspirational person on a much-needed topic in today's world.

—Shay Allie, barrister and author

This is an interesting and enlightening book that questions the essence of who we are and what we have trained ourselves to acknowledge and ignore!

Helpful advice and deep explanations throughout the book give you the knowledge and confidence you need to look at yourself in a different and more-positive world. Sit down, relax, and enjoy the book; you'll be a different person at the end of it.

—Antony Welfare, retail, e-commerce, and social-media expert

In *#Loneliness: The Virus of the Modern Age*, Tony J. Selimi attempts to address one of the biggest issues facing us in the modern world. He advocates that in a world in which we are seemingly so well connected through modern technology, the truth is that we have never been so disconnected with ourselves, and this is what lies at the heart of loneliness.

—Jo Hetherington, personal transformative coaching

Wow! Tony has delivered us yet another masterpiece. Tony has gone to a much deeper level to identify the inner segregation, the loneliness, and the disowned parts of ourselves and helped us break through to become our true, authentic selves. Tony is a visionary with profound, infinite wisdom; his message is nothing short of spectacular.

This book is a must-read for those who want to go deeper into their spiritual essences and uncover their true selves. The result—accessing your wisdom, developing sustainable wealth, and achieving long-lasting health—is priceless. Thank you, Tony, for this wonderful gift to humanity.

—Paul Miller, founder, Move Play Explore

Every one of us has experienced deep, dark loneliness at some point in our lives. However, with a loving family and great friends in my life, I didn't expect Tony Selimi's new book *#Loneliness: The Virus of the Modern Age* to be that relevant to me.

Tony's book is a wake-up call, a reminder that loneliness comes at us in many forms. Not only does Tony J. Selimi hold up our mirror and tell us where to look, but he also gives us interesting examples from his own and his clients' lives and valuable exercises and food for thought about how to see, address, and overcome loneliness. I recommend this book to anyone who is seeking a way out of loneliness and into living in oneness.

—Sandra Wick, Germany

Having read Tony's best-selling book *A Path to Wisdom* one more time, through great wisdom, he offers us the possibility to experience our true selves. He has chosen loneliness as a major problem of our modern time to bring us to realize we're interconnected spiritual beings having a human experience.

He shows us how we can make this experience joyful through real connectedness to our true selves or to make it dark and miserable through disconnection and solitude.

Once again, he offers us his unconditional love with his generosity of sharing his life experiences to make a difference in the world. The virus of the modern age is a threat greater than any other, taking humanity away from its true source of life: love, freedom, and connection.

—Dr. Rami Baz, Canada

This is a brave story. Uncomfortably brave and at the same time encouragingly open; it reassuringly nudges me to face the music and start writing my own score.

—Klementyna de Sternberg Stojalowska

Tony's new book, *#Loneliness: The Virus of the Modern Age*, takes you on a journey to connect with your authentic self. It also shows you how to connect with others and find your path to an inspired life. His compelling personal story touched my heart and inspired me to be more, love more, and speak my truth.

He shows you ways of segregation that create discord and pain and that lonely feeling within us that manifests in various forms in our society.

Read this book cover to cover and do all the exercises, and your body, mind, heart, and soul will be enriched. Pay attention as you read; in each paragraph, you will find profound wisdom that can help you transcend to new levels of awareness. A must-read book for today's modern citizen living in a technological Disneyland yearning for social inclusion, connection, and love.

—Patryk Wezowski, creator and producer of the movie *Coaching*

Tony's book about overcoming loneliness comes at the most significant time! We have been seeing a shift in people seeking more-balanced and fulfilling lives without knowing where to start! We are all victims of our own doing, which we think we cannot change, and we have to keep up our façades to protect our inherent beliefs.

This book beautifully helps us unravel the cause of our unhappiness, loneliness, and deep-rooted fear. It helps us master the multilayered beings we are to reach fulfillment and love of self; in so doing, we will inspire others to do the same.

—Melanie Le Roux, restaurant manager

I've lived for many years alone, lonely, and disconnected from the people around me. I used to imagine I had no choice but to live my life that way; I thought I would be in a permanent state of disconnection and loneliness.

Fortunately, that was not my fate. I happened across Tony J. Selimi a few years ago, and his work has reconnected me in a way that allows me to feel alive and connected in ways I've never felt before. Tony shares his insights, knowledge, and wisdom in a way that has helped me appreciate and realize how simple it is to find the point of connection and how we can all live connected, meaningful, and inspired lives.

We don't have to suffer from *#Loneliness: The Virus of the Modern Age*; we can instead embrace community and connection and reestablish ourselves with friends, family, and our environments in a way that serves us, our souls, and the wider consciousness of the world we live in.

Friendship, connection, and kindred spirits are there for us to experience, and with Tony's skillful weaving of his knowledge, wisdom, and expertise, his insights from his unique perspective, and his many thousands of hours of practice, it becomes clear that what we lack comes from within. It brought me to a point of realization that what I need to transcend the experience of loneliness and become as connected, nurtured, and loved as I choose to be resides in me.

If you have suffered in silence, alone, and without a friend or soul to turn to, embrace this book. You will discover what you have been doing to keep yourself from experiencing and connecting with others. Using the tools, exercises, and resources, you can shift to living a life in which you feel loved, connected, and free.

After I read this book, I was removed from the isolation that used to be my constant companion; loneliness became a distant relative I see rarely if at all.

Read this book and make the changes you seek in your life, transform your loneliness to connection, and make sure you learn how to use the TJS Evolutionary Method: the ALARM to break through all life's obstacles and permanently immunize yourself against loneliness, a virus of our modern age.

Thank you, Tony, for enduring your journey and sharing your wisdom at a time so prevalent as we stand on the brink of oblivion. The wisdom you impart directs us to creating a new reality, a new world in which together we create heaven on earth.

—Farhan Rehman, entrepreneur and social-media expert

Tony is more than qualified to speak as an authority on this subject. His life story left me breathless. Surprisingly, through all his adversity, he speaks with heart-centered accuracy that unleashes the power of love.

The fact that many of us are surrounded by people and constantly connected does not alleviate loneliness, but I believe this book can.

—Jenny Garrett, award-winning coach and author

At a gathering of entrepreneurs and personal-development aficionados in 2006, I was asked to share my views on wealth and connectedness. Why not? I was one of the most connected entrepreneurs in the country.

I felt like a fraud. Despite being so connected and appearing confident and happy, nobody had a clue that I felt alone, dejected and broke. I was dying inside, and there was nobody I could turn to. Or so I thought.

It wasn't until years later that I realized the extent to which most people were also hiding behind their façades. Like me, they were living a lie. Unfortunately, some fall into depression while others contemplate ending it all. At that moment, it matters not whether you are rich or poor, unemployed or a billionaire, man or woman, black, white, yellow or brown—nobody is immune.

Even though there is a plethora of information out there offering to help, *#Loneliness: The Virus of the Modern Age* is the first book to offer an in-depth examination and exploration of the causes of why people get to such a desperate space.

In this book, Tony J. Selimi has the reader spellbound from the beginning. He intricately weaves his real life and often harrowing stories with easy and practical steps to transform the pain and suffering. Those who read this book will quickly come to grips with how they have been blocking their own success and happiness in life.

This book is a rare gem; it's a wake-up call for those experiencing loneliness and the therapeutic professionals who wish to support their clients with processes that work. As a healer and an entrepreneur, I resonate with every idea and suggestion in this book, and I know it will with you as well.

Having had the pleasure of meeting and interviewing Tony J. Selimi on my radio show, I know him to be one of the most powerful coaches, healers, and spiritual teachers alive.

Once you've read this book as well as his first best-selling book *A Path to Wisdom*, you will understand why I and so many others have a deep love, trust, and respect for Tony.

I recommend you read every word in this book. In my humble opinion, the beauty of the book comes alive when you follow the exercises Tony suggests. Then you will experience true magic. Incredibly insightful reading!

—Harun Rabbani, entrepreneur, author, and founder of UnTangled FM

Now more than ever we have everything we need to live happier, more fulfilled, and more connected lives, but the tragedy is that so many of us feel lonely, rejected, worthless, and separated from happiness.

Tony J. Selimi has hit the nail on the head with this wonderful book by identifying how to immunize yourself against loneliness and by providing real-life stories and examples of others that will give you clarity and encouragement.

If your objective is to live an empowered, magnificent life, read his book and start your journey on a new path to awareness and joy. A treasure of a book for a world where everything is available at the click of a mouse.

—Shelley J. Whitehead, relationship, dating, and bereavement expert

I was first introduced to Tony J. Selimi and his best-selling book *A Path to Wisdom* at a special event Mirela Sula, the editor in chief of *Migrant Woman* magazine organized in collaboration with Regent's University in London.

Having read his first book, I knew this one would be even more special. *#Loneliness: The Virus of the Modern Age* takes us on a journey to self-reflect and unearth the many façades that give birth to loneliness, pain, rejection, and discord within ourselves.

Loneliness is a global problem; it's all around us, and yet we tend to ignore it. The effects are in every layer of our society, in the business world, in every government, and in every country, town, society, and village. It's in our personal and professional relationships as well as in our families.

He helps us recognize and understand these effects not only on our health, at work, and in our families but also on our global consciousness.

This book is full of real-life stories and scientific revelations and offers a road map of how to speak our truth, live in peace and in harmony with ourselves, with each other, and with our true nature. His personal journey through loneliness was mind- blowing, heart touching, and inspiring.

We often do things without ever realizing the impact they will have later on in our lives. Tony's transparent, authentic, and truthful words are lasting reminders of the healing power that speaking our inner truth has on our well-being, people we love, and the society we live in. Despite all the life adversities he endured, his words are infused with love, deep gratitude, and an invisible power to heal our deepest wounds.

Each chapter inspired me to eagerly take up the task. I felt I was taken into an inside luminous reality of connectivity at every level of existence. Reading this book will awaken you to the interconnectivity of all life and to the importance of the inner work required for you to be the change you want to see in this world.

In this timely and important book, Tony provides a solution for creating and strengthening the essential relationships that give our lives meaning.

This book will immunize you against *#Loneliness: The Virus of the Modern Age*, synchronize your body, mind, heart, and soul relationships, and help you embrace a connected, meaningful, and inspired life. Read this book with a childlike curiosity and you will heal your deepest wounds and pain, and live in love and gratitude.

—Baybars Altuntas, angel investor and best-selling author

Your emotions are never the problem; often, if not always, they are signposts to the problem. Here, with passion and care, Tony guides us a little closer to seeing our emotions for what they are—a potential path to healing. He shines the light of awareness and love on the dark places where many are scared to allow themselves to go.

If you are hearing the call for greater connection or feeling the pain that comes from not being true to yourself, this book is a gift for you. Learn how to embrace the parts of yourself you have disconnected from so you can truly embrace others free from judgment. With brave honesty and generosity of heart, Tony takes us on a journey through empathy to oneness, offering connection as the cure to the painful illusion of separation.

—Katharine Wolf, healer

Tony J. Selimi can be described only as an enlightened soul with a powerful, inspiring message. His story is one of a survivor, a warrior, and ultimately a heart-centered leader who by taking you through this book will give you a wonderful awareness that will transform loneliness and help you better understand life on this planet. Tony's book is both special and essential.

—Ayman Najafi, speaker and entrepreneur

In this book, Tony Jeton Selimi highlights the modern-day epidemics of individualism and loneliness, a modern virus causing individual disassociation with the self and the whole and the negative domino effect this is having on humanity and the world.

This virus has been subtly seeping into our systems; many are falling victim to it without realizing the diagnosis. This is a disease more prevalent in First World countries where, although we are more technologically connected, we have become more humanly disconnected. This book brings home to us the damaging repercussions our disconnecting has on the self and all humanity.

For those of us who relish our solitude, it provides a huge wake-up call to the detrimental effect this is having on ourselves and the world. Though many of us who feel a strong divine connection know we are never alone and thus do not acknowledge loneliness as a prognosis, it provides a gentle reflection of our shadow selves and highlights our disconnection to others and the toxic effect our seemingly harmless activities have overall.

In this book, Tony candidly shares his personal experiences and his deepest fears and pains and how from the ashes the phoenix rose. He provides a beacon of light for humanity to rescue itself from further disconnection and global meltdown.

With warm arms, he gently wakes us up to the reality we are creating and reminds us we are children of a divine master creator with unlimited potential above and beyond any computer. Our potential is forever evolving; we must therefore galvanize our connections with each other, support and nurture each other, and allow the evolution of humanity to flourish and thrive to realms currently unimaginable.

He provides an antidote to the modern virus of loneliness that if gone unchecked will have potentially catastrophic effects.

This is a wonderfully inspiring and uplifting book to guide humanity back to balance and healthy flow.

—Dawattie Basdeo, author and founder of Holistic World

As a coach who works with successful, time-poor executives and business leaders, I see the effects of loneliness all too often. We're entering a world in which the time for true connection is diminishing. The effect is an increasing sense of isolation and dissatisfaction with how we live; we are passing this on to future generations. Tony has identified and nailed this growing phenomenon. This book is an early wake-up call of our modern age and a book that is essential reading.

—Daniel Browne, author of *The Energy Equation*

Through my interactions with Tony, guidance from his theories, and the love that emanates from every word he writes, I have blossomed, rewrote my own story, and created a life I love. Tony understands the spiritual soul connection we all share. This connection, which Tony's writings have so graciously shown me, grants us all freedom from the pain of loneliness and fear. I've learned to love my true self unconditionally, and for this gift, I am eternally grateful.

—Gwendolyn Ann, natural health and wellness practitioner

Transcendence is where we are headed as a connected people and a planet. But first we must shine light on what is weighing us down and where we are disconnected in our hearts and with one another.

In this book, Tony J. Selimi gets to the core of one of the fundamental issues that affect perhaps each one of us, the globally connected consciousness, and our Mother Earth as a mirror's reflection.

We learn through this book how to stop poisoning ourselves and start thriving from within in a way that may relate and resonate with each of us on a deeper level. It's a level on which we are all connected but perhaps are also lost from. By simply reading Tony's words, we will naturally start soothing the aches of our separations and breaking the illusions that keep us feeling alone.

When I first met Tony, I was living in such an illusion; my reality was cold, dark, and lonely. On the outside, I seemed to have a lot going for me, but under the surface, I was empty, out of touch, and desperately trying to be more as a result of seeking to fill an agonizing hole that seemed to get only bigger the more I tried. But trying was all I knew.

At the time, if you were to speak with me, I would talk of how great my life was because I didn't know any different; I'd always felt alone. But after having worked with Tony J. Selimi and having undergone a journey through the TJS Evolutionary Method: the ALARM and the eight façades, I can look back and see the suffering and look in the mirror and see myself smiling a real smile and feeling full, balanced, and loving.

This connectivity now radiates out positively and impacts those around me through my work that embodies more creativity, authenticity, and love. I call this the ripple effect of divine wisdom I first encountered through Tony, who may well be the biggest stone thrown into the lake of our connected consciousness for a very long time and creating the most transformative ripple effects that will counteract our *Loneliness: The Virus of the Modern Age.*

—Adam A. Frewer, energy rebalancing coach

Tony's book is a real page-turner; each section calls up a memory or a circumstance I can relate to my situation or that of a friend. I've always felt there's a difference between loneliness and being alone, but I never acknowledged how these façades are like self-inflicted wounds that keep us from happiness.

Tony shows us not how to put a Band-Aid on truth but how we can acquire real skills to recognize and break down the barriers that bind us. I'm more consciously aware of my façades and can stop bad behavior in its tracks. Now I can't wait to sign up a friend to work with Tony too!

—Elaine Kennedy, Delicious Destiny

It is in-creditable, unthinkable, and unimaginable that Tony has been about to remain humble, grateful and hopeful throughout his heart wrenching life adversities that he openly shares to awaken us to the healing power of love and to our true being that resides in each one of us. #*Loneliness: The Virus of the Modern Age* represents who we were in our past, who we are in our present and who we may become in our future.

His illuminated insights give a glimpse of what the future of humanity may end up being if we do not take action now and become the custodians first of all of our body, mind, and hearts then of our neighbors, nations, humanity and our planet. To me, I see Tony more as gift of God, the light that we all need to find and walk the path that takes us away from the oblivion and into the oasis of elevated living.

I truly believe that if you to take the opportunity to see the light that Tony's path is showing, read this book cover to cover, and embody the wisdom it carries, you will rip the rewards that come with his amazing natural warmth, kindness, guidance and insights.

I am fortunate to have opened my scenes and comforted to be a client of Tonys' as well as befriend him. I love seeing first-hand the magic he creates. Yes he is different, yes he will challenge you to the core in a natural loving way, and yes he has made a big difference to my world and I know he will do the same to your world. Thank you and bless you Tony J. Selimi.

—Sue Bannister, MD of Cracking-Events Ltd

Successful on the outside, crumbling to pieces inside. This was my life before reading Tony's book and embarking on his yearly coaching program. My inner child was alone, chained, and screaming for attention deep in the cave of my solitude. I didn't know the discord within created emotional and physical pain, negative self-talk, and the many addictions that followed. I became a slave to my emotions, external circumstances, and people. Desperate to control everything in my environment, I hit rock bottom.

A year later, I own my power. I see the world from a balanced perspective, feel at peace with myself, and hold the reins of my life.

As a senior executive in a global organization, I observe that the same struggles endured as a victim of the loneliness virus are present in hundreds of thousands of employees, impacting every layer of businesses, their clients, and the communities they operate in. By applying the method that Tony shares in this book, I arise a sparkling phoenix. I believe through the embodiment of this work that corporations and individuals can achieve their inspired vision and become prosperous.

—Michele Scataglini, senior manager

#LONELINESS

THE VIRUS OF THE MODERN AGE

A balm for the restless soul yearning for connection, freedom, and love in the desert of emptiness.

—Dr. John Demartini,
international best-selling author

TONY JETON SELIMI

BALBOA.
PRESS

A DIVISION OF HAY HOUSE

Balboa Press books may be ordered through booksellers or by contacting:

Balboa Press
A Division of Hay House
1663 Liberty Drive
Bloomington, IN 47403
www.balboapress.com
1 (877) 407-4847

Because of the dynamic nature of the Internet, any web addresses or links contained in this book may have changed since publication and may no longer be valid. The views expressed in this work are solely those of the author and do not necessarily reflect the views of the publisher, and the publisher hereby disclaims any responsibility for them.

The author of this book does not dispense medical advice or prescribe the use of any technique as a form of treatment for physical, emotional, or medical problems without the advice of a physician, either directly or indirectly. The intent of the author is only to offer information of a general nature to help you in your quest for emotional and spiritual well-being. In the event you use any of the information in this book for yourself, which is your constitutional right, the author and the publisher assume no responsibility for your actions.

Any people depicted in stock imagery provided by Thinkstock are models, and such images are being used for illustrative purposes only.
Certain stock imagery © Thinkstock.

Author Photo by Dianna Bonner
www.diannabonner.co.uk

Print information available on the last page.

ISBN: 978-1-5043-4399-2 (sc)
ISBN: 978-1-5043-4401-2 (hc)
ISBN: 978-1-5043-4400-5 (e)

Library of Congress Control Number: 2015917815

Balboa Press rev. date: 01/22/2016

I dedicate this book to those souls who have felt the pain of being rejected or separated and felt different from what the perceived norm might be. To my loving mum Lutvije Selimi, and the many elderly people, children, and adults around the world who live alone and feel lonely, unwanted, unloved, and uncared for.

To all human being whose fears have led them down a path of deep loneliness and isolation and were subjected to the judgments of others and most of all their magnificent selves.

To all who may feel their lives are perceived as worthless, are willing to awaken to the interconnectivity of all life, and are ready to recover pathways to deep love, empathy, universal truth, and wholeness.

To every person deprived of food, shelter, knowledge, and nurturing.

To the people who give their time, energy, and hearts to care for the lonely, the elderly, and the abandoned.

To every spirit that has ever been, is, and will be.

To you wise souls who are learning, growing, expanding, and choosing to evolve so your inner light and love will shine and integrate the wisdom of your body, mind, heart, and soul.

Last, to my own spirit, who volunteered for this assignment, traveled through the cave of solitude, and continues to guide me to its ongoing unfolding and fruition.

CONTENTS

FOREWORD

Having known Tony personally, having seen him liberate his most empowered self during his attendance at my signature seminar program, the Breakthrough Experience, and having read his first best-selling book, *A Path to Wisdom*, I knew his new book would be something even more exceptional. He once again hit a home run for the human potential movement.

In *#Loneliness: The Virus of the Modern Age*, Tony takes us behind the apparent pain, rejection, and discord into a luminous reality of connectivity at every level of existence where we witness the core of evolutionary loneliness that's necessary in the process of recovering paths to deep empathy, social harmony, and wholeness.

His book is a compelling compilation of fascinating and enthralling discoveries that awaken us to the interconnectivity of all life. He weaves this together in a way that inspires each of us to eagerly take up the task. Tony's many years of deep, personal study, his depth of spiritual perception, and his academic background as a technologist have made him able to knit together the sciences, spirituality, and psychology with real-life experiences. He has taken what makes us human and turned it into a manual that helps us unpack and make sense of our apparent inner loneliness.

It's only in the illusive façades of our personae that we separate the inseparable, divide the indivisible, polarize the unpolarizable, label the unlabelable, and name the ineffable.

Tony provides a prescription for creating and strengthening the essential relationships that give our lives meaning. He's captured the deceptive nature of our false ego selves and introduced it in such a succinct and sophisticated manner as to leave readers empowered to take the reins and control where their lives are taking them.

In our hurried world, it's often difficult to create and maintain the kinds of connections necessary for healthy lives. This book is the balm for the restless soul yearning for connection, freedom, and love in the desert of emptiness.

Tony presents research that underlines both the importance of personal and social connections and the difficulties caused by their perceived absence; he helps us recognize and understand these effects not only on our health, at work, and in our families but also intellectually and in our hearts.

This timely, important book is much more than a description of the problem; it is a practical guide as well. Tony includes inventories for self-evaluation, outlines the path to enduring oneness, offers meaningful measures to improve our webs of support and social connection, and shows how we can become more confident, more connected, and more capable of achieving our intrinsic worth and more fulfilled in our day-to-day existences.

Filled with personal and other people's real-life stories and anecdotes and drawing upon spiritual traditions and teachings, science, technology, and modern psychology, *#Loneliness: The Virus of the Modern Age* is a timely guide to creating lasting, meaningful, and synchronized body, mind, heart, and soul relationships.

If, like me, you have spent a lifetime of learning, studying, traveling, and teaching and have a deep yearning to increase your understanding of life's greatest riches, you'll find reading Tony's book a most enriching and rewarding experience.

If you're experiencing rejection or loneliness or are going through any difficult situation, don't worry; Tony's gentle approach and subtle style weaves the most complex topics and the most cutting-edge science into easy-to-understand, bite-sized chunks that all will easily understand—be they personal-development novices or seasoned veterans of introspection and self-reflection.

Read this book with a childlike curiosity, and your life will be deeply enriched as mine already has been. Be prepared to go deep within and get to the causes of your apparent challenges—loneliness, abandonment, and rejection. Get ready to unveil your façades and tackle the source of the issues that arise from your inner discord; you will feel uplifted, inspired, and empowered when you finish.

You are left with a set of practical tools and solutions to help you get started on connecting to the essence of your being. Give yourself the best gift you could possibly wish for; read this book cover to cover to help you create a connection and order out of the chaos in your inner world. The journey this book will take you on is one of unlocking your inner wisdom and accessing the latent knowledge in your body, mind, and heart and the potentially infinite nature of your spirit.

Tony, once again you have cared, dared, loved, and shared a timely, transcendent message for the sake of all who are mysteriously bonded across the world.

—Dr. John Demartini, human behavioral specialist, educator, international best-selling author, and founder of the Demartini Institute

INTRODUCTION

Thank you for choosing this book to be your companion on a journey through which you will be able to demystify what *#Loneliness: The Virus of the Modern Age* is. It is my intention to help you uncover safe pathways for you to search deep and discover why you feel lonely, isolated, abandoned. Throughout this book my focus is to assist you in clearing away the resistance that makes you desire solitude.

Together, we will explore why we plant seeds of solitude that grow into concrete forests that isolate us from our essence and that of others. Learn what it takes to tap into the infinite being you are, the one who has infinite ability to grow, expand, change, manifest, connect, communicate, and love.

This is an opportunity for you to discover what scientific research has to say about the impact loneliness has on your physical health, emotional well-being, and your personal, professional, and social lives. It will bring to your awareness the universal, toxic effects loneliness has in your community, your family, your work environment, your finances, and in businesses across the world.

You will learn how to recover pathways to deep empathy, social harmony, and wholeness through finding your inner switch that turns on your inner light. That light can shine brightly and illuminate your way and can shine for all those around you in their journeys out of the isolation and into the oasis of connected living in peace and gratitude.

At the beginning of this book, I share with you transparently the traumatic life events that shook me to the core, stifled my sense of belonging, and led me to riding the never-ending emotional roller coaster of loneliness.

You will discover what it took for me to go from being rejected, fearful, abused, bullied, uncertain, abandoned, and unloved to living in gratitude and embracing wholeness. I'd love to share with you how I went from being a homeless teenage refugee of war to being a director, entrepreneur, and a best-selling author.

Along the journey, you'll come to realize the healing power of gratitude through the tools that acquire the knowledge and wisdom of the ancient sages as much as that of philosophical scientists. Once you apply this in your personal circumstance, you will shift your current reality to one more favorable, inspiring, and aligned with your soul's vision and mission.

Think about this book as a collection of stories, facts, and applied knowledge that are all true. These stories shine light on the personal impact that loneliness had on me and has on each one of you as well as the grief impact it has on the collective consciousness. Each story or metaphor I share illuminates the reasons why addressing loneliness now in some cases will change your life and could even save your life.

From every story shared, you will draw practical knowledge, tools, and the wisdom required for you to overcome your loneliness and be better equipped to deal with life's adversities. It offers you a solution to change your life, awakens your hope and inner genius to help you through troubled times, and instills the beliefs required to assist you in your soul's evolution.

Something on every page of this book will make you realize how thirsty your soul has been for your attention and love and for finding another, more-favorable way of looking at the world.

Come to your own conclusions on how, despite all the advancements we've achieved so far, we continue to forget the simple but very important power of contact. Without contact, there is no connection, no flow, no light, and no life. The lies we have been fed, the skewed perceptions of who we think we are, and the lack of contact described throughout this book give birth to loneliness.

See how the absence of contact with the higher mind creates the many discrepancies the lower mind creates between the ideal and perceived self and how this discrepancy gives birth to seeds of separation and loneliness.

To be lonely often reflects the hunger of your soul for a different way of being with others and for a different way of life that currently might not seem possible to you. It's the distressed feeling that occurs when your personal, social, professional, financial, and spiritual relationships are less satisfying than you desire.

This book describes how loneliness is perceived, conceived, and measured; how loneliness is mentally, emotionally, physically, spiritually, and financially represented; how it influences your thoughts, feelings, and behaviors; and how its consequences occur in all spheres of your life.

An increasing number of people around the world feel isolated in their little cocoons. They feel lonely, unloved, unwanted, uncared for, and disconnected because of their painful reality. We have become so busy, so distracted, and so disconnected from our true essence that we no longer even know who we truly are.

In her observations during her visit to the United States, Mother Teresa gave an American reporter a very bold statement that describes #*Loneliness: The Virus of the Modern Age.*

> The greatest disease in the West today is not TB or leprosy; it is being unwanted, unloved, and uncared for. We can cure physical diseases with medicine, but the only cure for Loneliness, despair, and hopelessness is love. There are many in the world who are dying for a piece of bread but there are many more dying for a little love. The poverty in the West is a different kind of poverty—it is not only a poverty of Loneliness but also of spirituality. There's a hunger for love, as there is a hunger for God[1].

---

[1] The quote was used with the permission of the Mother Teresa Center, exclusive licensee throughout the world of the Missionaries of Charity for the works of Mother Teresa.

This bold statement is a great mirror that reflects how far we've evolved in material wealth, technology, and our outer understanding of life and how ignorant we are in our understanding of our inner worlds, our infinite natures, and our souls, the main pilots of our lives.

Each chapter, each bold statement, each word in this book is an invitation from your soul to you to stop, rethink, and reassess who you truly are so you can connect to your essence, your truth, and your spirit and embody a new way of living and being.

Though we have created the most advanced technologies known to humanity with the potential to connect us to every human being on our planet, this book alongside Mother Teresa's statement is a great reality check and reminder to us all that life is far from the truth we have created for ourselves.

You don't need to read it in a book, be told by a friend, or experience an adversity to know that feelings of loneliness, rejection, and separation are painful and unwelcome. Your body's innate intelligence will trigger the alarm that will warn you when it's in a state of imbalance or discomfort or in a threatening situation. Your body doesn't feel good about being subjected to pain, shame, or any emotions triggered by loneliness. The problem and the truth of the matter is that despite this knowing, very few people are listening and doing something about it before it's too late.

You too may have left home, walked into an elderly-care home, children's refuge, or a place for homeless people and seen, felt, and experienced how lonely the lonely can be. No matter what you have or don't have in life, feelings of loneliness, rejection, and abandonment, as well as feeling not listened to, uncared for, and unloved is common to us all.

This separation, isolation, loneliness, and disconnection follow you in every sphere of your life. On your daily commute to work as well as in airports and restaurants, you'll see people glued to their mobile phones, iPads, tablets, computers, and laptops in desperate attempts to connect, communicate, and be heard. Yet if you look around, you'll see many people ignoring the presence of others right next to them, failing to create a personal connection with them, and shying away from simple conversation.

Technology and social media have become frantic attempts to numb the loneliness that some of us feel and suppress the pain that comes from feeling rejected, not listened to, unacknowledged, or unloved for who we truly are.

Those of us who have become so distracted with life's daily demands fail to see that if we continue living that way, we are bound to become even more isolated, selfish, and self-centered.

If you don't do something about it, you may become an emotionless robot that's programmed by a central control unit and told what to do. The possibility of someone creating advanced technologies as seen in movies such as *iRobot*, *Kingsman: The Secret Service*, and many others is real.

Imagine what our world would look and be like without harnessing the power of nature that provides us with air, water, electricity, fire, and gas. It would be impossible to invent any of the modern technologies we now have and have become accustomed to. We take for granted radios, mobile phones, TVs, satellite communications, computers, laptops, tablets, robots, planes, and the Web that have helped us create rich content and share trillions of bits of information with people around the globe.

Similarly, without the contact, connectivity, and communication that occurs between the cells in your body, you wouldn't have been born and been able to function. Your internal organs wouldn't work. Your mind wouldn't be able to make decisions; you wouldn't be able to follow your feelings, know right from wrong, or hear your intuition. We as a species and the world as we know it would cease to exist.

This is why I felt deeply inspired to share the message of this book with you all. This message carries the healing power of love, which can support you in your journey from feeling lonely, abandoned, or rejected to being connected to your essence, your empathy, freedom, and your compassion.

By facing life's adversities head-on, honoring your truth, and experiencing quantum awakening, you can harmonize your body, mind, heart, and soul. In doing so, you will connect to the love that descends from the higher realms of existence. When you make contact with love, your curiosity will awaken, your heart will open, and your soul will be free to be.

A profound feeling of internal discord and your desire to seek a greater significance and connection in your life is what brought you to pick up this book. Rest assured you have come to the right place to learn, grow, and be the creator of your life.

It's a lifetime endeavor to awaken to the truth of who you truly are, embrace all you are, reestablish the harmonious flow of love, and restore the mental, emotional, physical, and spiritual balance you need to live life aligned with your highest values and potential.

Choose now to achieve connectedness, balance, and flow in the shortest possible time through everything I share in this book. The more you enjoy this journey, the more you'll be able to extract the lessons, learning, and wisdom I share in these pages.

Decide now to walk away from this book having learned as many lessons as you can. Facing each experience and using the TJS Evolutionary Method: the ALARM helped me access a place in myself that is quiet, peaceful, and in harmony with all that is. Having achieved this state of balance, I saw how changes in my inner state of being rippled into world around me as I started to be of service to many people around the world.

As I reached this beautiful, blissful, internal state, I realized the human potential I had and that I had created many façades over a lifetime that were hidden from my conscious awareness and buried deep in my subconscious.

The more curious I became, the deeper I dug and the more I discovered hidden lies I had perceived as truths. The more I dug, the more I found unused parts of myself that I started to remove. Doing so enabled me to unite my inner state of being to the outer experience of life, hence forging a oneness with self.

I broadened my understanding of life through the process of curious enquiry, surrendering to adversities, and investing a significant amount of time, money, and energy in my personal, professional, and spiritual development.

The more I learned how to navigate the ocean of feelings of being abandoned, rejected, uncared for, and lonely, the closer I got to the island of balance and paradise.

If you don't awaken to the truth of who you truly are and honor your role of being custodians of your body, mind, heart, and the planet we all share, you'll continue to live your life on snooze and in the shadow of your own magnificent light.

Each chapter is a call from your soul, a call for love that will awaken you so you connect, unite, and love in one voice and with one heart. Should you ignore this call, you'll continue to unconsciously contribute to global wars, epidemics, terrorist threats, addictions, increased divorce rates, social isolation, depression, suicide, obesity, and loneliness. You will ultimately suffer in silence.

This call for love from your inner being is awakening many of you to the importance that connection, truth, and love play in our lives. It's a call to bring your unique gifts to the world so you too can inspire and give hope to the hopeless, the lonely, the rejected, and anyone who has ever felt the pain of being uncared for, unloved, and unaccepted.

I wrote this book from that call for love; I want it to become the lightbulb in your head that shines brightly and illuminates your path to help you navigate the dark parts of your mind and the busyness of your noisy thoughts so you can find your own path to wholeness, fulfillment, and an inspired life.

Every page of this book is your personal assistant that can bring clarity to your confusion, help you feel more connected, show you how to reach inner peace and harmony, and enter a state of flow. These are required for us all to unite and accept our uniqueness.

The experience gained from the many paths I have walked gave birth to this book and my apparent loneliness. Each path I took offered its own challenges and lessons; each situation presented to me on these paths created some form of isolation, loneliness, and rejection. Each person I met on these paths, each situation, and each adversity was my teacher; they showed me something different about myself. I thank and love the people who caused me tremendous pain and the people who brought pleasure to my life and showered me with their love.

Removing the façades you carry daily will allow you to unveil your narcissistic and altruistic parts that have been with you for many years. For some of you, this process in itself can be uncomfortable as it creates new loneliness that comes from missing and letting go of the things you're familiar with.

Take time to go in yourself to seek, find, and reflect upon the answers to the questions laid out for you in this book. See which part of your life is craving your attention, what fears you haven't dealt with, and what you're yearning for and not giving yourself permission to have, do, or be.

The ability to learn from all the separation you may have experienced in life may be a highly selected trait, but it can no doubt be greatly improved by guidance, as this book will show.

The adversities I faced were the catalysts that changed my perception of the meaning of life and death. Through hardship, we tend to lose touch with who we truly are and create the illusion of being separated from the ocean of oneness. These are illusions that come from the pain of being rejected, not listened to, unloved, and uncared for that sometimes come from simply being in the wrong place at the wrong time. For some of you, the loneliness, pain, and separation you face may also come from being born into this physical reality with a genetic disease beyond your control.

Each of your life challenges will have its own pains, struggles, lessons, and opportunities for growth and will allow you to yield your wisdom. All these are dimensions of your experiences of disconnection and connection and will be represented in one form or another in this book.

My aim through this book is to help you transmute your loneliness and all the challenges you face throughout your life into blessings that will give birth to situations that make you rethink, reassess, and reconnect to what matters in life.

You'll discover in our journey together how this is an essential part of healing your loneliness, how to overcome the difficulties that may seem a mission impossible, and what you can do to change your life. This was certainly the case for me and for the many clients I have helped.

Research shows that many people become inspired, healthier, and more productive as they feel loved, nurtured, and connected with their true selves, their spirits, and their hearts. This is your opportunity to switch on your inner light and remain in a state of great health, balance, and calm.

Scientists and quantum physicists tell us how on a subatomic level, everything is interconnected in our universe and how we too are cocreators of this universe. If, like me, you love science, you may know through studying quantum physics that a particle at the subatomic level can coexist simultaneously in two places at once. With that knowledge, we can easily assume that we too coexist simultaneously across multiple dimensions.

Your job is to learn how to harness the knowledge and wisdom that governs the universe and our existence so you can reconnect outside the realm of time and space to parts of yourself that coexist across the many dimensions and learn and grow from the infinite wisdom of your soul.

Over the coming chapters, you will see how my calling has always been to bring peace where there is war, to bring hope where there is none, to bring freedom where there is fear, and to be the light to those living in the dark and feeling disconnected, rejected, and alone.

This book gives you the tools to overcome your apparent loneliness and any other life adversities you may be facing. It will help you plant new seeds that will grow into the essential ingredients you need to live a connected, meaningful, and inspired life in which you will embody the infinite wisdom of love in your relationship with yourself and your significant other, in your parenting of your children, at work, and in everyday life as a leader in the world.

The busy lifestyles and daily pressures you face force you to spend more and more time searching for tools that can help you to cope better and do more with less time while feeling content, calm, and reconnected to your true nature.

As you go through this journey, you will start to understand how essential it is to own the disowned parts of yourself to live in oneness. When you do so, you will start to envision a fuller life and closer relationships, you will become a more loving parent, you will work in a spiritually conscious and alive workplace, and you will embody authentic, heart-based leadership. This is what I have achieved in my life and help my clients realize, and I believe it's possible for you to do the same!

Raising the awareness of who you truly are will increase your vibrational frequency. The higher you vibrate, the more flow there is in your body, the more your heart opens, and the more your loneliness will be transformed into a beautiful state of love, contentment, and inner calm.

This is your opportunity to be immunized against loneliness by coming to a place in yourself where the possibility of making the choice to change exists and to learn how to access the control switch that turns on these choices.

Although some of the stories in this book come from my own experiences, in many instances, I am only the narrator who relates events that occurred in the lives of some of the extraordinary people I have encountered: clients, family members, friends, colleagues, and people from all walks of life I've had the good fortune to meet.

With the permission of my clients, I used their real-life stories to illustrate points. I have changed some names to protect the privacy and identity of some of them. I have always loved stories and gained a lot from them. We're all wired to learn from stories. That's how experiences have been recorded and communicated since the beginning of time.

Some of the sections in this book will speak to your heart and mind. They can move you, and when you're moved, you're likely to learn lessons from them. I spent many late nights channeling this book by connecting to the infinite ocean of wisdom that many of this world's inventors, philosophers, scientists, healers, teachers, and prophets have connected to before me.

This knowledge will take you on a deep, personal journey. If you give yourself permission, you'll yield the greatest rewards that come from expanding your self-perception. If you've once loved with your entire being and at some point felt the pain of being abandoned, rejected, abused, and alone in that love, you will know how painful that can be.

The way you feel ripples into the environment; it affects the people around you and has a toxic effect on the global consciousness as well. Through self-reflection, you will come to your own conclusions about why immunizing yourself against loneliness is that important and how in doing so you can stop this separation within from rippling into your environment and other people.

Along the way, you will encounter powerful questions and exercises to help you break through your fears and your body's current conditioning and overcome obstacles that prevent you from being connected and from living a balanced, healthy, meaningful, and inspired life.

Doing all the exercises in this book will help you get clear, show you how you can zoom out of your current way of seeing life, and allow you to observe it from your higher mind's, your soul's, perspective.

You picked up this book because you are eager to break through your loneliness and expand your mind and awareness so you can get to that place in yourself where you acknowledge how amazing you already are. Go beyond your imagination and what you may currently perceive the interconnectedness of all life to be. I invite you to come on a journey with me and explore the true nature of your loneliness this book describes.

This is your opportunity to see a completely new world through a new pair of lenses. You will gain a fresh, different, enriching, and accepting point of view that will honor the infinite nature and the wisdom of your spirit. It's up to you to commit to and maximize your investment in this book and in yourself. Granting yourself the gift of time to complete all the exercises herein will yield the maximum benefit for you.

Congratulations on following your intuition, reasoning, and your heart's true voice by picking up this book and choosing to illuminate your mind, open your heart, and elevate your existence.

—**Tony J. Selimi**
International Best-selling Author,
human behavioural and cognition specialist

CHAPTER 1

MY JOURNEY THROUGH LONELINESS

Many of my life's adversities you'll read about all happened to me at a young age and resulted from plain bad luck and things outside my control. Some misfortunes, as you'll come to understand, came from my being in the wrong place with the wrong people at the wrong time. Other difficulties came through the choices I made from a place of pain, shame, and guilt and from not speaking or honoring my truth. I didn't know what my true values were, the importance the values played in making those choices, and the decisions I made for the things that I sought in life.

You may be at a place in your life where you are aware that through times of pain, adversity, and struggle, you have the capacity to yield the gifts and riches worth harvesting. Or you may be at a time in your life when you're finding it hard to let go of the pain, shame, fear, and loneliness that accompany those experiences. Unbeknownst to you, they may have become your constant companions and the best friends you don't really like but can't do without.

What I am about to share here are the life events, situations, pain, shame, and loneliness that silently and craftily entered my life. They became my best friends I deep down disliked; they were my constant shadows I couldn't get rid of. You know exactly what I'm talking about here—the disowned parts of you that have the power to keep you in the shadow of your light.

But they are the parts of you that, if understood—not judged—and accepted for the roles they have played in your evolution can help you unlock the treasure chest buried deep inside. Once opened, the treasure chest unleashes the leader, the doctor, the scientist, the problem solver, and the creator you were born to be. The creator who knows how to nourish the body, unlock mental faculties, navigate the ocean of emotions, and get you to the island of star-like living.

As you are about to find out, reaching the place whence I am bringing this gift to you wasn't easy. Many hungry sharks craved pieces of my flesh. I spent many sleepless nights praying to an invisible man called God for love, acceptance, and freedom from the pain, shame, and feelings of being different. These were the feelings I grew up with that accompanied me into adulthood.

Yes, I shed many tears, I faced many fears, and I went through many violent storms that destabilized my being. All that happened to me was under the blanket of a normal, hardworking, loving family that was unaware of the hidden pain, shame, inner discord, and guilt that had started in me at a very young age. It was a time when I just wasn't aware of what was truly happening and the impact it would have on my emotional well-being and physical health and the way it would shape my future.

By going through each of the twelve major life adversities you'll read about, I came to understand the darkness and appreciate the light in me. I became the person I am today in possession of the knowledge, wisdom, and tools to help many others from all walks of life liberate their imprisoned souls, pursue their hearts' desires, and live meaningful and inspired lives.

I now know that the journey I went through was essential; it freed me from the resistance that had been built up in me from early on. I was able to reconnect with and honor the disowned parts of me and reunite with the soul that was always there but had never been given the power to just be the free soul it was.

For you to have read this far, your soul must be yearning to find out more about how it too can liberate itself and help you be free with your love. I thank you for coming on this luminous journey through the compelling, personal, and traumatic life adversities that damaged my sense of belonging. I'll share with you the many life situations that led me to feeling I was riding in every carriage of the longest roller coaster of life called loneliness. No matter which carriage of that roller coaster I was in, I was always greeted by the many spin-offs of loneliness—I felt abandoned, rejected, separated, unworthy, unheard, bullied, fearful, invisible, unappreciated, and most of all unloved.

From a very young age, my constant companions were adversity, a curiosity to know why, and the feeling I was different from my family, my friends, the religion I grew up in, and my classmates.

As you read about my emotional roller coaster ride, I'll share with you the pivotal moments in my life that challenged me to my core and allowed me to arrive at the place I am now, where I'm connected, loved, and liberated from the shackles of loneliness and embraced by the love that lives in every cell of my body.

THE BABY WITH CROOKED LEGS

Throughout my life, I've had many physical health challenges. The first one presented itself the day I was born. I was born with crooked legs. From what I can remember, for almost three years after I took my first breath, I couldn't stand or walk. My deformed legs caused my hardworking parents distress and presented them a challenge; they had to work long hours to provide for six of us, and I know they did all they could to help.

In today's world, parents have all the support they need to correct what's now considered a normal birth defect. Back then, my hardworking mom did what any mother would do; she followed the advice of her elders and used what means she had to straighten my legs.

I remember crying in pain when my mother would daily tie my legs up tight in an attempt to straighten them. Sometimes, my sisters or my grandmother would find time to take care of me, but often, due to her having to work long hours at a restaurant, I was left alone in a cot unattended for hours.

Despite the daily pain, I endured. I remember curiously observing the world and wondering how everything functioned. Although I wasn't able to walk as every other child could, I faced the pain with courage and the deep knowledge that my mom would fix my legs and make me free to walk, run, and play like every other child.

I spent a lot of time in pain and alone, tied in a cot. As the time passed by, somehow, despite the odds, my mom succeeded in her mission to correct my legs using her nurturing, motherly instinct.

I was finally able to walk freely and unaided. I started enjoying what most children did in the early '70s. I played outside and learned to ride a bike; I appreciated my newfound freedom. I never realized until later in life the impact that stage of my life had on me.

The next few years passed by very quickly; the pain I had experienced turned into pleasure. During that time, I learned many practical skills that came from living on a farm in Macedonia with my sisters and grandparents and from working with my parents in our restaurant in Zenica, Bosnia. I learned how to cook, clean, and feed the animals. I learned the alphabet, three languages, and math. I leaned to value money and appreciate my parents' hard work. I give my thanks and love to my mom, grandparents, sisters, brother, uncles, and everyone else who was present during that part of my early-life journey.

THE ABUSED CHILD

If having crooked legs wasn't enough, the next adversity that impacted me the most happened at age six, when I was sexually abused by a young employee who worked for my dad.

He was hardworking, smart, and good looking, and he was always smiling. I enjoyed his company. He'd take care of me daily; he treated me to ice cream, he took me on walks, and he taught me how to cook and use the equipment in the restaurant. One day, he took me into the storeroom where we kept all the vegetables. When I came out, my life was never the same.

Back then, I knew little of what was right and wrong. I didn't know what had just happened or that it would change my life. I ran out of the storeroom crying and feeling ashamed and afraid. I went straight to my parents to tell them about the inappropriate behavior. I felt helpless, shamed, abandoned, guilty, and in pain. He had told me not to tell a single soul; he said that if I did, my parents would disown me for the shameful act, that God would punish me, and that I would go to hell.

I stood there in front of my parents, tears streaming down my cheeks, trying to tell them what had just happened, but I wasn't given a chance to speak a word; my parents were busy with the customers. As was often the case, I was sternly disciplined and reminded that the customers and the business were extremely important and always came first. They told me that it wasn't the right time to cry, that instead, I should dry my tears, grow up, be a responsible member of the family, and help them out.

Although I was desperate for their ears, their love, and their protection, I did as I was told. I stopped crying, pulled myself together, and went around the restaurant to clean the tables.

From then on, I learned to live in shame. I learned to put on a façade, pull myself together, and appear strong while deep down I feared for my life and felt lonely, abandoned, rejected, disgraced, and scared it would happen again.

From what I can recall, when my family wasn't around, he'd find me, take me by the hand, and find ways to trick me into going into the same room. Each time I left it, I was filled with more fear, shame, and guilt. I blamed myself for what was happening and felt dirty, afraid, and used.

Most nights, I would cry myself to sleep. I confided in God, the only one I could talk to, the one who didn't judge me, the one I prayed to and asked to help me and take that man away. I believed my turn would come and my wish would be granted once God had helped all the other people who needed him more than I did.

Despite all the pain caused by what was happening, I comforted myself by telling myself that I was lucky, that I was better off than many children around me. I was well dressed and cared for, and I came from a hardworking family that gave me a lot of love. I was well fed and had a great home, and I knew God would ultimately respond to my prayer and send his army of angels to take that man away.

My mother instilled in me a belief that God always answered our prayers, and he did. He didn't send his army of angels. Instead, a miracle happened. One afternoon, the man took me to the room where we had a machine for making dough. That time, he told me to be silent and not go anywhere because he had to prepare dough before my parents returned.

He told me not to move until he had finished loading the machine. He slammed me hard against the wall, and I felt a sharp pain in my back. I had hit an electrical switch as I was thrown against the wall. I remember screaming as I'd never screamed before. I was in the most physical pain I had ever felt. As my back hit the switch, the machine turned on, breaking that man's arm into many pieces. He shrieked loudly in pain before the safety switch was activated.

Everyone came into the room. Seeing his broken arm, they turned their attention to him. They looked at me as if I were to blame. That made concrete the shame I was already feeling, and I ended up feeling guilty and responsible for what had happened even though I was just six. I was scared about what would happen next.

I was listening to everyone arguing about whose fault it was and why I'd been allowed into the room in the first place. I was in shock, crying, and very afraid my parents would find out about the things that had happened in the storeroom. I felt ashamed, afraid, fearful, hurt, and confused. I tried to make sense of why this had happened to me with this man, what I had done to deserve it, and why I couldn't tell a soul.

That man didn't take me to the storeroom again. I knew God had heard my prayers and had granted my wish. The man was dismissed.

From then on, I never entered the storeroom again or any other closed, dark spaces. From that moment on, I was claustrophobic and fearful. I was afraid that he would come out of the dark and punish me even more than before.

After that, I could never fall asleep in the dark, and I didn't like being alone. My family made sure there was a light on in the room so I could sleep. Sometimes during the winter, we wouldn't have electricity, but my mom or sisters would make sure a gas lamp or a candle was by my bed to keep me company until I'd fall asleep.

The trauma of this experience left me deeply wounded, scarred, and segregated. It triggered long-term amnesia that for many years I was completely unaware of.

Later that summer, my parents took me to Gostivar, my hometown, so I could start school in September. I was approaching seven, and I started spending most of my time at our farmhouse with my youngest sister Drita and my grandparents Akik and Satka. I'd go to Zenica, Bosnia, the place where the abuse had happened, only during school holidays.I loved going in Zenica, as it was where my parents were working, spent most of their time, and where I kept learning so many wonderful skills that I now know prepared me to handle all the life adversities that followed.

On the other hand, living on the farm with nature and with my younger sister was amazing. I was very happy to do my chores, work the land, look after the animals, and sell our produce in the market and in the gypsy community that lived near our farm.

I learned how to milk cows, harvest wheat and corn, pick cherries, apples, and pears, and keep bees. I also did extremely well at school.

Since I remember, I was always self-aware; neither my parents nor my four sisters had to tell me to do my chores or finish my homework. I was surrounded by many friends who spent most weekends with me at my home. Upon reflection, I think that was due to my fear of being alone.

To my parents and the outside world, I was a happy, loving, and supportive child. But deep inside, I knew I had a buried secret. I knew there was something troubling me that like a virus kept spreading through my body.

In the next journey, I'll share with you what happened next.

STRUGGLING TO STAY ALIVE

When I was nine, I was hospitalized due to severe pneumonia, a heart murmur, bacterial infections, and many other immune-related illnesses. In total, I spent just over two years in hospitals feeling alone. I was isolated from my family, friends, school, and everything I loved and enjoyed. The freedom I had felt after my mom had managed to straighten my legs so I could walk was very short lived.

As my health deteriorated, I started to have near-death experiences. I would observe my body from above my hospital bed. I was floating in midair. I saw everything that was happening, and I heard all the conversations taking place around me and everything my family said when they visited me. I saw what my mother was doing and the way the nurses were treating me. At some point, I learned I could go through walls and see everything happening in the hospital. That was the first time I truly came to understand there is life after death.

When I was in less pain, I seemed to easily get back into my body. Being bedridden, I learned much about pain, being alone, and suffering in silence with no one to help. Despite being very ill, I considered myself fortunate; my mother was at my side. She spent most of her time by my bedside, as did my eldest sister, Feleknaz, who was at university and had just started to date her then-boyfriend and now-husband, Xhavit. I was blessed to have a visit from a family member every day. However, I observed how so many people in hospital had no one who would visit, nurture, and care about them.

During that time, I was heavily medicated, and I gained a lot of weight. I had been slim, but I became a balloon about to explode. While I was still able to walk, I'd visit and talk to the doctors, nurses, and the patients who were lonely and had no one to visit them. I knew just being next to them, talking to them, and telling them jokes helped them feel better, cared for, and nurtured.

After I had spent a year heavily medicated in the main hospital in Gostivar, my parents were told that I was too weak, that I wouldn't make it, that I had a maximum of a few weeks to live. I recall floating above my body and seeing my mum praying over my body just the way I used to when I was praying to God to make my former abuser go away. It was heartbreaking. I told myself to go back into my body and that way not leave my mum or my family alone.

My parents, having cured my brother from epilepsy by alternative routes, turned to the esoteric world of spiritual healers, priests, and imams for help. My mum went to many sacred tombs to pray, and she lit many candles.

They decided to take me to the main state hospital in Skopje, Drzavna Bolnica, where better medical professionals might be able to save my life, but my family continued to work with spiritual healers.

A year passed. Despite the doctors' orders to rest, when I would feel better at night, I'd sneak out of my room and visit patients suffering from cancer, leukemia, pneumonia, and heart illnesses.

We were all treated with so many variants of serious medications that I often wondered why some of us got better while others died. The hardest thing was to see every day someone passing away and seeing families crying and being separated from their loved ones.

I acted as if I were a doctor. In my heart, I knew my mission was to help people heal and extend their lives. When I had out-of-body experiences, I often wondered if it was what people called heaven. If so, where was God, and why was he not here with me healing all these people who prayed to him daily?

One thing I was sure of; my out-of-body experiences happened when I was in the most pain. At the time, the only conclusion I could come to was that my out-of-body experiences were natural occurrences when my body was in pain and fighting disease.

I eventually started to get better. I was more and more in my body, and my body started to heal. I felt better day after day. I knew that praying and being taken to various spiritual and faith healers made me feel better, and once again, I was fully in my body and awake.

Through all the in- and out-of-body experiences and from observing so many ill people, I learned about how illness, loneliness, and the fear of being sick could be healed through hope, prayer, and facing adversity head-on. I learned how having certainty, communicating with love, and listening to people's stories made me and the people I was with feel better.

As I got better, my parents were given doctors' orders that I must continue with a special breathing therapy and that I needed to spend another year in a famous children's hospital in Ohrid, a very beautiful and culturally significant town in western Macedonia.

The hospital was by beautiful Lake Ohrid. I continued my healing journey there with top medical experts and received weekly injections of Extencilline. The fresh air, breathing clean oxygen, and other medications would help repair the damage that had been caused and strengthen my weak immune system, heart, and lungs.

I arrived at the hospital and was taken to a room, shown my bed, and introduced to more than twenty other boys who were there for various health reasons. That evening, I met the night-shift nurse. Though he was only going from bed to bed to distribute medications, I froze. My whole being went into shock. I recalled the painful images of my sexual abuse. I knew he wasn't what he seemed to be.

That same evening, when it was time for my medication, he came to my bed and asked me to lift my T-shirt so he could measure my heartbeat. At that moment, my entire body shook violently in fear. I couldn't look into his eyes. I started to cry. I asked for my parents to come and take me home.

That night, and every night from then on, the lights would eventually be switched off. Through the darkness he would emerge. He would grab certain boys by their hands and take them to his room. I could hear them cry and scream. When he returned them, I saw how they would cry silently, physically paralyzed by fear.

Witnessing these boys being forced to go with this man and hearing their cries lifted the veil of my amnesia. It brought back vivid memories of my own abuse in the storeroom.

Fear took over my body. I stopped sleeping and eating. My condition started to worsen. A few days later, my parents were called in and told that if I didn't eat and take medication, I had little chance of making it. When my mother arrived, she tried hard and used emotional blackmail to make me eat and take my medication. She wanted me to stay there.

That time around, I had no intention of backing off. I told her how every night, after everyone went to sleep, I saw the night nurse come into the room and take a boy back to his room. I told her that after a while, they would return upset, crying, and in pain. I'd hear the boy's silent screams, the screams I recognized very well, the screams I had let out each time I had been taken to the storeroom years back. The boy would return to his bed after a while, when I was sure he wouldn't return. I would go to his bed, cover him with the duvet, and hold his hand as he silently cried. I told Mum I had to be strong for him, I had to protect him. Once again, since no one would listen, I would pray to God to save him as he had saved me.

My mum took me in her embrace. She was confused. She cried for a while. She told me she would sort it all out. She called the doctor and told her about the incident. They brought the nurse into the room, and of course he denied any wrongdoing. He told my mother it was his duty to make sure children took their medication and to use any means necessary to make the children comply. He also said some drugs could have an effect on sleep and cause hallucinations. He said that children often told lies so they wouldn't have to take their medication.

This time around, my mother followed her instinct and told the doctor that she knew her own son, that I was fearing for my life. She insisted on moving me to another room with a different night nurse.

The moment my mum left, I knew that if I didn't run away, the man would come after me. I spoke to a few other children about the screams at night. Many wouldn't say anything, and others were fearful, but a few of them confirmed that they too heard the voices and a few of them had been taken into the room. Some children who had been there for a long time were convinced they had to do everything the male nurse demanded they do if they wanted to receive their medication.

By that time, a week had passed. I learned where every door and exit from the hospital was and when there was a security guard change. At two o'clock on one Sunday morning, I escaped. I never wanted to return.

The next day, I was found asleep by the lake and was returned to the hospital by a woman on her way to work. I woke up in the same bed from which I had escaped. I saw my mother crying next to me. I told her if I didn't go home with her that day, I would never eat again. I said I'd rather die than be one of the boys who would be taken into the nurse's room when the lights would be switched off and everyone was asleep.

That was the first time I felt my mom had truly heard me, listened to me, and took me seriously. She removed my hospital clothes, took me in her arms, and gave me a long hug. She emptied my hospital cupboard and gave away all the food to the rest of the children. She took my hand, and we went to the doctor's office.

She insisted that she wouldn't leave me there, that it wasn't safe for me to stay there. She asked the doctor for my medication and injections; she said she'd have our family doctor give them to me at home.

That was the end of yet another life adversity that created another mask behind which my fears and loneliness lurked, where my views about how unsafe the world was and my many negative beliefs about life and the world resided. But I had to be strong for my family and myself.

I was happy to be free again with my family, go back to school, and enjoy playful times at the farm with my dog Lux.

BULLIED AT SCHOOL

Having spent so much time in hospitals, I took every opportunity to learn as much as I could so I could help all the people who were ill, who were suffering, and who had no one to care for them. I've always had a strong desire to study science, physics, astronomy, geography, biology, chemistry, math, languages, and computers.

My father always instilled in us the importance of education. Although two of my sisters studied medicine, he wanted to have a son become a doctor, as back then it was considered the most reputable and prestigious thing to do. Neither he nor I knew that I wouldn't become a medical doctor but would grow up to be a world-renowned author, coach, and healer who helped heal many people's emotional and physical pain and their broken hearts.

I finished primary school; at age fourteen, I started high school at one of the best math schools in Skopje, the capital of Macedonia. From that age on, I lived on my own and have ever since been fully independent of my family.

I lived in Karposh 2, an area on the main boulevard, Partizanski Odredi, in a studio flat my parents had bought when my eldest sister, Feleknaz, started her university degree.

During the next four years, I was the man and the wife of my own life. I cooked, cleaned, and looked after my own place. I had a part-time job working as a waiter, I studied hard, and on the weekends, I'd go to my farmhouse in Gostivar and help my sister and grandparents with chores. All the skills I had learned in the restaurant helped me in my day-to-day life.

During my high school years, I won many awards and competitions in math and physics. I was a happy teenager; I was curious about learning. I had a zest for life and was considered by many to be one of the best students in all the schools I had attended.

Despite all my academic achievements, loneliness, rejection, and feeling different continued to be my companions throughout high school.

I was living alone and away from my family with no one around me to protect me from predators. As a young teenager I faced bullying at the hands of some of the Macedonian teenagers in my class who did it for the pure reason that I was of Albanian ethnic origin and studying in a 99 percent Christian Macedonian school.

This bullying didn't came just from some of my schoolmates; it also came from certain teachers who, despite my excellent academic background and always answering every question, refused to give me high scores until the end of the school year. That was when some of my teachers who had witnessed my achievements in various school competitions and events and had seen that I had won prizes for the school would question other teachers about my low scores in their subjects.

I was subjected daily to verbal and emotional abuse because I was not of Macedonian origin. Back then, we didn't have Google to ask and learn the meaning of the names I was called. I would ask my parents and family members why they were calling me names, or occasionally, I'd see these words used on TV or when people would fight in the streets.

Throughout my four years at high school, despite the fact I was studying very hard and was considered one of the top ten students, I started to experience anxiety, depression, loneliness, unhappiness, and poor sleep due to daily bullying.

Making the issue worse was the fact that my emotional response to the bullying often went unnoticed by my classmates and the head teacher; I felt the need to conceal that I was being bullied. I didn't want to make it worse, and I was embarrassed to tell anyone because I didn't want to appear weak, as if I weren't man enough to deal alone without my parent's helps with life's adversities.

Unaware of all I know now, I responded passively to bullying. I was always anxious; my self-esteem and confidence were low. I became quieter in class and focused on my academic success. The bullying went on for four years unabated; it was my daily hurdle. I never knew what the boys would say or do any one day.

What kept me strong was my great relationship with my family. I looked forward to spending time with my youngest sister Drita, and I knew four years would pass fast. I had a bigger dream to pursue. If the dream was meant to happen, the bullying wasn't going to stop me. It made me even more determined to succeed. I was blessed; my parents believed in my academic abilities. My sisters were as well interested in academics but not my brother. He was happy to take over my parents' restaurant and make a living that way.

My parents valued our becoming educated, increasing our knowledge, and in going to university so we wouldn't end up like them working 24/7 and away from our children as they had been. My father instilled in us the desire for knowledge, education, and a better, nine-to-five lifestyle early on. Just as many parents did in those times, they sacrificed a lot for their children. My parents worked hard to provide us food, clothes, education, and a great home because they wanted the best for us.

During my high school days in Skopje, my next-door neighbor Todor was a university math professor my dad hired to tutor me. I learned the math and physics he taught at university up to the master's degree level.

I learned that not all Macedonians were nationalists who hated Albanians; many were just as good as my family. During high school, my tutor's family became my second family; I felt nurtured and supported, and I learned the importance of acceptance and not putting people into categories.

Having a private tutor throughout high school helped me earn top marks and be ahead of all the students in my class. My dad's investment in my tutor helped me achieve top scores on the entrance exam for one of the top engineering universities in Zagreb, Electro Tehnicki Fakultet (ETF). I remember feeling joy and happiness when I called my dad and mum and told them I was holding my letter of acceptance from the university. It said that my scores were the highest and that I was among the top three of thousands of applicants who had applied; only 120 were accepted yearly.

The hardship of living alone, being bullied for four years, and feeling rejected by some of the students and teachers at high school created in me many façades that only later, when I started the inner work of peeling them off, made me realize how they had impacted my physical health and my emotional well-being.

TEENAGE SOLDIER OF WAR

In summer 1988, having just graduated from one of the top math schools in Macedonia, I moved to Zagreb, Croatia's capital, to further my education. I found a flat and a part-time job working in a club as a barman. Though I was alone with no family around me, I felt the happiest kid on the planet as I was studying at one of the top engineering and science universities in former Yugoslavia.

That euphoric journey lasted less than two years. In 1989, civil war broke out and spread rapidly to other parts of the country. Many other students and I were conscripted by the Yugoslav army to fight a civil war I despised; I was being forced to fight the people I loved. An emotional volcano grew in me that was ready to explode at any moment and destroy everything in its path. I once again felt alone. I was far from the people I deeply loved and reluctant to fight a war my entire being despised.

As the time went on, I saw many atrocities committed by the newly formed Serbian National Army as well as by the Yugoslav state and the army that was meant to protect its people.

As the conflict spread in other parts of the country, I realized the people's army I grew up to believe in wasn't what I was experiencing. Loneliness, fear, and feeling different from everyone else were like weeds that took over me and caused negative emotions. I was forced to do things that weren't aligned with the values I had grown up with. I felt the pain of every soldier and every civilian who was subjected to the "ethnic cleansing" mission of the Serbian nationalists. I spent fourteen months living in fear, in survival mode, alone, scared, constantly threatened, and not knowing if I would live.

But during my months of service, I developed a very close relationship with the captain I reported to and his wife. He had no sons or daughters. I spent much of my free time with him and his wife, and I was his trusted chauffeur. Over time, I became the son they'd never had. By that time, I had lost contact with my family; soldiers couldn't use the telephone lines.

As the civil war spread in Croatia, my captain, a true believer in the old Communist regime, knew it was only a matter of time before it spread into Bosnia and the rest of the country. He knew that the army he had once believed in was disintegrating and had become a tool for the Serbian nationalists to fulfill their own mission.

He called me into his office one morning and said, "Tony, you completed your duty a long time ago. The army I once believed in is disintegrating. It's not a safe place for any of you. Many of your comrades at the front are being killed. Each time you leave camp, I fear I'll never see you or any of your unit alive. It's time for you and what's left of your unit to go home to your families."

He issued a discharge order the same day the war spread from Croatia into Bosnia. Many of our comrades had already lost their lives in the conflict in Dubrovnik, Vucovar, and other parts of Croatia.

He helped us cross the border into Macedonia and advised us to get out of there as it would be the next place where the war would spread. Just as he predicted, within a year, the conflict reached there as well.

As the war spread, so did the fear, uncertainty, and atrocities. Macedonia became unsafe, so my mum again saved my life. Due to the war, she couldn't get in touch with dad as he was in Zenica. She borrowed money from our neighbor, and the next morning, my cousin Burhan and my mum drove me to the airport and bought me a ticket to London, where I would be safe until things calmed down.

I remember crying all night on her lap. She cried too. As I checked in at the airport, we saw in each other's eyes fear, love, and uncertainty of what the future held for us. We wondered if we would ever see each other again. I was torn between the desire to safeguard her and her wish for my safety.

She hugged me, kissed me, and blessed me as I was passing passport control. She waved and told me to not look back. Her last words were, "You're a survivor. Don't worry. You'll be safe. I love you. Make us proud!"

It was heartbreaking to once again be separated from my family, not knowing if I'd ever see them again. I kissed the land as I boarded the plane. I knew it would be a long time before I returned.

I cried throughout the four-hour flight to London. All I could think of was the family and friends I was leaving behind. Many of my friends had died in the war; many in my family were trapped in war zones. My loving mother had once again saved my life, but I felt helpless. I was emotionally broken. I couldn't stop thinking, *Will I ever see my family again? Will I ever feel my mum's loving embrace? Will I ever be normal again after the suffering and the pain I've endured?*

Somehow, against all odds, there I was at London Heathrow. I was fearful. I had no place to go, no friends, not much money, and I could hardly speak English. The immigration officer checked my passport; he asked me what I was going to do in the UK. I became brave. I told him that I was going to study engineering and that I wanted to make a difference by helping people around the world heal their pain.

He smiled. He told me I had great ambition and a big job ahead of me. He stamped my passport. In his nice English accent, he welcomed me to the UK.

HUNGRY, HOPELESS, AND HOMELESS

With the £250 in my pocket my mother had given me, a small rucksack full of basic belongings, and a bag of food my mum had cooked for me, I made my way to central London.

I exited Piccadilly Station. I was alone in the middle of a big junction. Thousands of people were around, minding their own business; I was alone with no one to turn to. You can imagine how traumatized, lonely, and small I felt.

I made my way to Trocadero. I'd been told that I would meet Albanian people there in similar circumstances who had fled the war and that they would help me find a job and a roof over my head.

That evening, no one showed up. I found a hidden space where no one could see me and slept until morning. The morning came and went. I waited for a week for someone to show up, but the longer I waited, the more hope I lost and the more fearful I became. My food started to run out. I moved around, but I found no one who spoke my language. Days became nights, nights became days, and I slowly accepted the fact that I was alone in a big city I knew nothing about.

For a while, I lived homeless, penniless, and fearful on the streets. I slept underneath bridges, in parks—any place that could offer shelter from rain, wind, and cold. Back then, I knew nothing about any social support or benefit system. Once again, I felt at the mercy of God and my mum's belief I was a survivor.

At age twenty, I was living on the streets of a big city. I felt uncared for, abandoned, and rejected; I had no one to talk to. I spent most of my days crying, longing for the war to stop, and hoping for the day when I could go home to my family.

Having just spent over a year in a civil war, I knew that the loneliness, the fears, and the challenges I faced homeless in the streets of London where nowhere near as bad as the daily challenges I'd had back in the war zone. But when you have no money, no friends, no roof over your head, and no one to turn to for help, a big city like London can be the loneliest place on the planet. Despite all the fears and the uncertainties that came from living homeless, from feeling the cold in my bones every night, I knew that I had to remain humble, grateful, and hopeful that things would get better.

During that time, I lost all faith that the situation at home would get better. The civil war spread to other parts of the country, and the situation worsened. I had no means of getting in touch with my family, and I started to lose my sense of belonging and identity.

My heart knew there was no going back anymore. My heart knew that I had to make it, that I had to pull myself together, do all I could to get a job, get a roof over my head, and take care of myself. I had lost at least ten kilos on the streets. I looked as if I had been in a concentration camp.

I knew that if I didn't do it, no one would do it for me. The country I once knew was being destroyed by the hour, and the Yugoslav passport I had became invalid as Yugoslavia ceased to exist as a country. I had no home to go to, no identity, no contact with my family. I didn't know if I would see them again. I felt emotionally destroyed. I spent many nights crying as I hit rock bottom.

I couldn't see a way out of what then seemed an impossible mission. I prayed each day. Deep down, I believed I'd be okay. I knew that the worst had passed and that from then on, things could get only better.

And they did. Eventually, my path led me to meet my first friend, Enisa. She offered me a place to stay in her Earls Court flat for a few days until I found a job and accommodation. She wrote down the addresses of a few employment agencies where I could register for work. Within two days, I found a job at an Italian restaurant and a small bedsit in Shepherds Bush to live in.

I felt so happy, grateful, joyful, and full of hope. Once again, I knew my mum's prayers and my belief that things would turn out okay helped me meet the right person, get a job, and find a place to live. I love and thank Enisa, one of the first to help me get my life back on track.

A year later, my hopes of returning home had vanished. My country had disintegrated. TV news reported daily of people dying. It was not safe for me to go back. I made the trip to the Home Office in Croydon and applied for refugee status.

It took eight years of constant battle with the Home Office before I was granted refugee status. I never understood why it took so long for that office to grant a war teenager refugee status. For eight years, I felt I was living in no-man's land, alone. Each visit to the Home Office was another scratch on the wounds I was trying to heal.

Millions of people at home were losing their lives. The whole world knew about the atrocities happening in Croatia, Bosnia, Kosovo, and Macedonia, but I was kept in limbo, in the dark, and always told they needed more evidence before they could grant me refugee status.

Living in limbo for almost eight years helped me address my many insecurities and emotional blockages and go beneath the many façades I had built up due to my feelings of fear and abandonment. In the process, I freed myself of many fears and attachments to material possessions; I learned to survive with very little while remaining true to the values my parents had taught me.

Despite all my challenges, I remained focused. I continued to work hard, I learned how to speak and write English, and I enrolled at university. All the adversities that had come my way taught me something different about myself. I gained many wonderful skills, and I built trust and confidence in myself and developed self-understanding. I learned how to function effectively in my new environment.

EXISTENTIAL GENESIS

You can imagine how thrilled I was when I got a job and a place to live. I felt safe for the first time in a long time. Although I hated being alone, I was grateful to be alive and healthy.

To accomplish what I'd told the immigration officer at the airport I wanted to accomplish, I needed to pay for the education I needed. I needed to find more jobs so I could enroll in an evening course to learn English for business.

Throughout the '90s, I spent much time crying, alone, and longing to once again experience what it felt like to be a normal kid with a family and time to enjoy life. When I was on the streets, I saw many parents with their children. I'd smile and try to remember what it was like to be with my family. I'd try to recall the love, the laughter, the arguments, the feeling of being safe, warm, and loved with my family.

I found other jobs besides the job at the restaurant. I worked an average of eighteen hours a day at three to four jobs. I knew I was being paid below the minimum national wage, but I was grateful for the work. The more I worked, the more people I met. My desire grew to continue my education, become successful, and help others overcome loneliness, abandonment, and other life adversities.

I spend my free time and hard-earned cash on evening and weekend courses to learn English. Within two years, I learned to read and write in English. Zoe, one of my teachers, recognized my potential and encouraged me to continue with my education. I enrolled in a two-year course at the City of Westminster Adult Education Centre in Paddington and completed my Higher National Certificate in Electrical and Electronic Engineering with Mathematics with the highest grades possible—straight A's.

The next two years passed even faster. I worked and studied full-time. Despite all the tears, the solitude, and the fears for my family in the war zone, I once again told myself to be strong; I knew there was sunshine after the rain.

My commitment, consistency, and hard work started to pay off; I excelled in all my exams. I got an award from the mayor of Westminster for achieving distinctions in all my subjects and for being an exemplary student at Westminster City College.

Perhaps you can imagine the emotional roller coaster I was on. It had taken time, energy, and effort to get to that stage in my life. I learned the healing power of gratitude; it opened new opportunities for me, and my awareness of what I could do with my life expanded exponentially.

Mr. Dobson, who taught math at Westminster College, helped me further recognize my potential. Despite the fact I didn't have refugee status at that point and I could not attend the university for free, I was determined to work and do as many long hours as it takes to be able to pay for the university fees required. He believed if there was anyone who'd be able to succeed, it was me. I was the only student who had straight A's despite the pain, the worry, and the uncertainty I suffered. He encouraged and inspired me to continue my education. His energy, frankness, and belief in my abilities were the same I knew my dad had for me and every human being.

Other tutors saw my talents, recognized my abilities, and encouraged me to apply to the top four universities: Imperial College London, University College of London (UCL), Cambridge, and Oxford. Mr. Dobson helped me fill out the university application forms to apply to the four universities. I remember telling my teacher that it was a waste of time, that only the children of the rich aristocrats had a chance to study at these world-renowned institutions; I told him, "I'm nobody." He smiled and said, "They and England should be proud to have children like you. You'll get an offer. I believe in you."

That night when I went to sleep, I turned to God, the only one who listened to me and kept granting my wishes. I needed his help.

Six weeks passed quickly. I continued to work twenty hours a day, and one night when I got home, I opened the door to my Notting Hill flat and saw a letter waiting for me. My heart beat faster. I opened it. There it was in black and white and verified by a signature. Once again, my wish had been granted. I had been accepted by three out of the four universities I had applied to. I chose UCL to study electrical and electronic engineering as well as management studies.

I put my hand on my heart, closed my eyes, and thanked God. I cried for joy, but I was sad because I wasn't able to share the news with my family. But the next day, I shared the great news with my tutor. I saw tears of inspiration flow from the eyes of someone who believed in me and was as happy as my father would have been.

He took me out for lunch to celebrate and asked me which school I planned to attend. I said that though I wanted to attend Cambridge or Oxford, I'd have to attend UCL for practical reasons. I would have to work full-time to pay the fees. I had to be close to my three jobs, and UCL was the closest.

He smiled, congratulated me, and told me in his black African accent, "Tony, you are a fine, young, wise man." We finished lunch. He gave me hug and smiled. He said, "I believe in you, Mr. Selimi. You are like a sun that always shines even when it rains. You've had a lot of rain in your life, so fly above the clouds, feel the warmth of the sun you are, and hold on tight. Get your degree and live an extraordinary life." That was the last time I saw him. I thank him and all those who supported me on my journey back then.

I started my degree, life took over, and I worked three jobs to make my dreams reality. Despite burning my candle at both ends and dealing with all the life challenges that came my way, I was happy, grateful, and thankful about how far I had gone from living on the streets to attending one of the top UK universities and pursuing an engineering degree. The miracle I was creating was due to the values and skills my parents had taught me, my determination, hard work, and most of all to God and his angels who were always there to help, guide, and support me.

For sure, there were many more life challenges that are worth mentioning as well as having been abused, having been a teenage war veteran, having been separated from my family, and living alone in a big city. Though it all, I felt lonely, different, and abandoned. Many of my fellow student friends used to socialize regularly, but due to my exceptional circumstances, I wasn't able to enjoy my student years as they did theirs. I had no time to socialize, and that made me feel isolated, alone.

Three years passed very quickly. I graduated with honors and had my diploma in hand. In 1998, eight years after the civil war had broken out,

I received a great blessing. I was reunited in London with my father and a short time later with my mother.

I was over the moon; I was proud, grateful, and happy, and I felt the sunshine my tutor had told me I was radiating from the center of my heart. I was alive and reunited with my parents. I found myself with my father having a graduation dinner at the Ritz with a few close friends and their proud families.

Despite fear, loneliness, and many other negative feelings, I had learned how God, hard work, and fortune had put my parents exactly where my heart wanted them to be, with me celebrating in style at the Ritz, where the rich and famous—the likes of Princess Diana—wined and dined. I counted the many blessings that had come out of my painful life experiences.

The more grateful I became, the more blessings came my way. The next big blessing came to me the same year when out of the blue I received a letter from the Home Office enclosing my UK citizenship certificate. I finally had a new place to call home and a new sense of belonging. I once again had the freedom to travel and visit the rest of my family.

After graduation, I landed a job as an IT administrator for Traffic Directors for London. I also continued to work evenings and weekend at Harvey Nichols, Harrods, and Cannons Sports Club to save money for a deposit to purchase a flat.

A year went by. I kept praying to God, and yes, my dream came true. I bought a lovely studio flat in Pimlico; I finally had a home to come back to. For the first time since I had left my family, I felt the warmth, joy, and happiness of having my own home, my own roof over my head. I was safe. I had income, friends, and an identity. London became my new home. I thank all those fortune put in my path during that time. I wouldn't be the person I am today without their love, care, guidance, and support.

As my finances improved, I started traveling the world and visiting all the places I had grown up in. I went home to pay tribute to the friends and family who had lost their lives during the war. If I wanted to move on with my life, I had to make peace with what had happened and with my past that was always following me like a dark shadow.

Throughout my journey, I had lived through many lonely moments, shed many tears, and faced many adversities that fueled my feelings of being separated, fearful, and abandoned. But I continued to pray, forgive those who trespassed me, and kept learning more about who I was and what I was here to do.

My zest for life grew; I learned more skills that helped me grow and face each adversity head-on. I learned from people of many cultures and made friends wherever I traveled. I became even more curious about the mysteries of life, science, and how the universe works.

A voice inside was nagging me to learn more about life, who I was, and the mission I was here to accomplish. It was the mission I'd had since I was that six-year-old, abused child who wanted to be heard, help other children be safe, and heal the emotional and the physical pain of the many people he had encountered in hospitals.

Although I had no idea then how I could ever achieve such a noble act, I had an overwhelming desire to help those in need; my heart opened up each time I helped someone. The pain I had felt became the power engine of my life; it became the sunshine my grandfather, father, and my teacher at Westminster College told me I had. That sunshine was always there, radiating, shining, and sending heat and light energy required for life to exist.

I spent the next fourteen years working long hours and building a very successful IT career. I learned many wonderful skills and attended many professional development courses. I met people, learned more skills, and was great at creating calm in times of panic, clarity in times of chaos, and certainty in times of distrust. I was able to get people to work as one and to always see the bright side of life.

I was working as an IT consultant for major government sectors on many technology projects as well as full-time in the retail industry implementing infrastructure upgrades, B2B and B2C systems, sales-force automation, and consolidation of back-end and front-end systems and technologies. I maximized investments in technology by connecting all the companies' departments—sales, marketing, HR, IT, and finance—to repairs, manufacturing, and all the customer systems and data. I continued to grow in my career and gain promotions. During that time, I took many professional IT courses that helped me climb the career ladder and become a better leader.

I was also fascinated with the esoteric and the psychology of the human mind; that led me to study many disciplines. The many books I read and the courses and seminars I attended helped me expand my knowledge of myself.

I studied psychology, neuro-linguistic programing (NLP), cognitive behavioral therapy (CBT), life coaching, the Demartini Value Determination Process, the Silva Method, the Sedona Method, kabbalah, and quantum physics. I learned the secret and the law of attraction, Eastern healing concepts such as Barbara Ann Brennan's Hands of Light, meditation, Buddhism, shamanistic healing, and Martin Brofman's Body Mirror system of healing.

In the process, I overcame the many of my childhood-abuse issues, fears, anger, and lack of self-confidence, self-worth, and self-love. I gained immense knowledge, insight, and tools that helped me heal my body, mind and heart.

THE RISE OF THE PHOENIX

During this time, while my life was taking off, I faced a major sexual identity crisis that impacted my well-being, destabilized the foundation I had worked so hard to create, and created a huge separation between my family and me.

I wanted to avoid the pain, the shame, and the loneliness that came from being gay and born into a Muslim family and into a society that condemned those who were different. I felt pressured, unloved for who I truly knew I was, and unaccepted. I believed that to fill those voids, avoid the shame, and satisfy my family, I had to get married.

Having done so much personal development work on myself, I started to believe that if I could heal the many aspects of my life, I could change my sexual orientation, which I believed had something to do with my early childhood abuse. I wanted to be what everyone told me I should be, a heterosexual who needed to marry, have kids, and be a loving father.

My marriage, however, created another painful experience that impacted me and everyone I cared about and loved, including my ex-wife, whom I will always be grateful to and love for being the angel who paved my path to honoring and accepting my true identity.

From a very young age, I learned to subordinate myself to my parents and other people's values and fears. I learned to hide behind the masks I had built to protect myself from predators, shame, and others' needs and expectations of me. I made many life decisions that were well intended but ended up creating more pain, separation, and feelings of rejection. Getting married was a decision that shook me to the core and created the greatest segregation I had ever experienced.

I had grown up suppressing my sexuality; I had lived with the pain of having been sexually abused and being homophobic. I wanted to be the "straight" son my parents and family had always wanted me to be. That was the façade I had hid behind all my life; I was afraid to take it off for fear of being rejected, unloved, abandoned, and uncared for. I was in many ways the same shameful boy who had entered that storeroom.

I had been groomed to be what my parents, religion, and the society told me I should be—a good, straight son who would marry, be a great husband, and look after his mum in her old age. I believed in this falsified vision of self until I started to give voice and listen to what my body, spirit, mind, and emotions were telling me about myself.

The conflicting voices of my two personae caused painful feelings of inner separation. I was torn between being the son who loved his family and respected his religion and culture. I desperately wanted to please and honor my mum and dad, the people I so loved, missed, adored, admired, and had huge respect for. But deep down, I knew I was gay, different; I enjoyed the freedom this part of me had.

As I continued in my quest to dig deeper within myself, I realized I was trapped in a self-made prison. The more fears I was uncovering, the more the voice in me that loved me for myself started to disappear. It became like a fading SOS coming from a sinking ship. As time passed, I stopped listening to it; I wanted it to go away. The other voice, the one with fears and deep-rooted, subconscious beliefs that had been with me from birth, started becoming the dominant voice.

This deep hunger, desire, and thirst to fit into the heterosexual world I was expected to belong and conform to led me to create a false identity and a reality in which I would feel safe, loved, accepted, and the man my parents told me I was meant to be.

I started my journey to become heterosexual and started to seek help from various professionals who claimed they could help change my sexuality. That journey led me to creating a perfect life and the illusion to wanting to get married, have kids, and live happily ever after.

With the help of many therapists I talked to, priests I confessed to, and mosques I prayed in, I left the cave of loneliness created by my secret gay life; I felt strong enough to make the shift. I had faith in God, in my family, who kept telling me how much they loved me, and in my newfound belief that everything was possible. But instead of helping me create the miracles I was promised by many people whose help I sought, my faith left me even more alone, trapped, and fearful.

I was convinced that with all the personal and spiritual development I had undertaken with myself and many people I saw, I could change myself. I thought I could be like every heterosexual man I stumbled across whom deep down I secretly admired. I was told to find a wife to love, have children to nurture and play with, and fulfill my parents' wish for me and look after them.

I decided to shut down all my gay feelings, thoughts, and lifestyle and disconnect from most of my gay friends I loved and was loved by. I was told that was necessary for me to do so to become the heterosexual my family expected me to be, the one deep down I too wanted to be.

I didn't know the damage this would cause to my mental, emotional, and spiritual self. This fake truth planted seeds that made me want to change myself and finally get rid of the deep-rooted homophobia instilled in me by the people I loved. Or so I thought.

When my last gay relationship ended, I decided it was the sign I had to be what I was nurtured to be. I spend a year in solitude and at some point felt I was ready to meet a woman like the mother I adored; she would become the love of my life and the mother of the children I so desired to have.

Of course, God and the universe listen. I ended up finding a beautiful woman to date. I told her the truth and my desire to change my life. She was extremely supportive and loving. The more time we spent together, the more we fell in love with each other. After a year, we were engaged; we wanted to get married and raise a wonderful family.

For the first time, my life started to make sense. I could be close to my family, do family things again, and have a sense of belonging, a dream, and a mission to fulfill my parents' birth-given destiny for me. I felt I knew what I wanted. I believed that my childhood abuse had had something to do with my being gay and that changing my sexual orientation was possible.

I didn't realize how my spiritual ego was growing at the same speed as my awareness of life, love, and the workings of the universe. Giving my power to something outside me brought me to a point in life that I felt getting married was the right thing. It was time to lock away everything I knew about myself in the deepest ocean of my subconscious and honor my parents', my culture's, and society's values and wishes. To achieve this, I had to put to permanent sleep the voices of my own wants and needs.

I willingly let myself be taken to many so-called gay-cleansing professionals and spiritual teachers and to the sacred places that as a child helped me heal from life-threatening illnesses to be "cured" of my gayness. I changed my gay life; I suppressed my sexuality. The voice I heard was that of my mother and my family's wishes for me. But deep down, I knew I was living a fake life, a life that didn't feel natural to me or one I belonged in, a life that led me to the deepest ocean of solitude.

Although I told my fiancée, my sisters, and my friends about the way I felt, I was never really listened to or given the opportunity to express my wants and needs. Though they told me they loved me, they also said that they would never accept me being gay and that the only option for me was to continue to work it out. I thought it was the only way to be loved and accepted by my family.

During that time, I felt alone and misunderstood. Part of me died every day. The more time passed, the more the voice that knew the real me got angrier, louder, and stronger. The two voices in me started fighting for their existences. You can imagine the destructive power that two competing voices have; they threatened me with the destructive power of an atomic bomb. This same destructive power can be observed in nature when water and strong wind come together. My conflicting voices came together and started to destroy everything in my way.

The more I kept trying to be heterosexual, the more my entire being rejected it. I didn't enjoy or belong in a heterosexual lifestyle and community though I desperately wanted to belong; nonetheless, I tried hard to fit in.

I was grateful that my parents had instilled in me strong morals, values, and beliefs about how relationships should work. All the things I was experiencing came from the same beliefs I held dear. The life I was living came from a place of not honoring my truth, lack and fear and the need to be validated and loved.

Honoring my family's values was more important to me than learning, listening, and honoring my own values. In time, my anger and pain grew as did my awareness of how the source of my homophobia was my feeling of unworthiness and inadequacy and my subordinating myself to my family, religious, cultural, and social values.

Despite the fact that for many years I had lived in London being free and openly gay, I didn't know the power those subconscious beliefs, morals, and values held over me. They made me make decisions that created havoc in my life and the lives of those I cared about and loved. At that point, the other voice was stronger than my authentic voice. I couldn't accept my own truth, the one that came from my heart, soul, and entire being. No one in my family would love me if I honored it. Being gay and enjoying love in the arms of a man were at the same time painful and pleasurable experiences. They liberated while they imprisoned my soul.

I stopped listening to my voice. I denied my emotional guiding system and disconnected from the gay world in London in the hope I could change my sexuality and honor my family's and my own expectations of how my life should be.

I didn't realize how my internalized homophobia and the deep hatred I had for myself had come from being born into a family that couldn't accept and love me for the person I was. Instead of listening to my feelings, honoring my authentic self, and honoring my values, I chose to listen to the voice that told me to please others, love others, and put others first.

That voice wasn't new; it had been with me for many years. I observed how my family would judge everything I was feeling and tell derogative jokes about gay people. Despite knowing I was one of those people they joked about, the pain I felt and the shame I carried forced me to continue to honor and live my family values. I was told it was the right thing to do to be accepted and loved and be part of the family. It was their way or the highway.

That battle continued every day. My own voice became an echo I could hardly hear. Deep down, I loved the voice I tried hard to silence, but I never turned it up to give it the strength it required to be heard.

You might relate to this story on many levels. It might remind you of your hidden truths that perhaps you're afraid to speak about, the fears you might have, and the choices you made from a place of need, lack of self-worth, and wanting to be accepted by the people you have strong ties to.

I hope this story inspires you to reflect on and learn the source of your feelings of separation and identify your true voice, the voice of your own alarm ringing in you to alert you about things in your life you may not be paying attention too. It's a quiet voice that might be telling you something about yourself. Close your eyes. Listen. Hear the voice of your being. Let it come into your conscious awareness, allow it to just be, and be open to what it's trying to say to you.

Open your eyes and write down everything you're experiencing. You'll find this exercise useful as you continue to learn about the façades you must unveil to open the doors that conceal your light. Through your light, you will open gateways to loving, learning, and living your truth and being one with your heart, mind, soul, and life.

When ready, come back here and let me share with you what happened next. As you can imagine, I reached the deepest part of the cave of wretched solitude with no exit in sight. I had no spiritual food, oxygen, or water. I had no one to turn to for help.

I finally got married. I had an amazing wedding. Everyone who loved me was there, and my mum was extremely proud. Everyone was very happy that I had finally come to my senses and had married.

That was when I totally separated myself from the truth I had locked deep in a part of me no one would ever find. I had found a beautiful woman who came from a good family, and I was ready to continue my legacy and meet all my family's expectations.

After the wedding, after everyone had left, my bride and I were driven in a white, beautifully decorated limousine to my home. My first night with my wife was the moment I faced my worst fears, the truth I had tried to change, and the reality of my body rejecting everything my mind had created.

The moment I first lay in bed with my amazing bride, I realized I would never be able to fulfill the expectations of the marriage and the heterosexual life I had desired and had worked so hard to create. I had spent so much time, energy, and money to come to the moment I had been prepared for since birth, yet on the first night of my marriage, sadness, darkness, and fear enveloped my heart.

My inner voice told me I had made one of the greatest mistakes in life. I was in a room with a beautiful and desirable women who loved me deeply, who had taken a chance on an abused boy desperately wanting to find happiness. Yet my heart knew I wasn't able to give her what she had married me for: my love, heart, soul, and all the commitments and promises that came with marriage vows.

Days turned into weeks, weeks into months, months into years. The illusion I had created due to feelings of separation, fear, and rejection turned me from being loving, open, successful, cheerful, and full of life to being lifeless. I was dying inside from the pain caused by my inability to fully love my wife. The light I had shined on those I loved and the world since the moment I was born started to become dimmer until total darkness enveloped my being.

Many of you may have experienced how one decision, one thought, one belief, one intention shifted your reality and created the illusion into which you sunk or from which you soared like an eagle.

During the day, I loved my wife from the depths of my heart. I played the role of a good husband and son; I did everything to fit into the environment and with the people I grew up with, loved, and held dear.

However, as evening would approach, darkness would take over. No matter how much I tried to fulfill the intimate needs of my marriage, I failed repeatedly to be the lover I knew I was and wanted to be.

This pain of not being able to love the person who had sacrificed her life for a chance for us to be happy drove me to physical illness. As you will find out later on, it drove me to attempt suicide. Each evening, I would hear my inner self-critic and my suicidal thoughts, and I thought the only way to end my pain and the suffering the two of us were experiencing was to take my life.

I was in a toxic environment; I couldn't face the fears, the consequences, and the judgment that came from those who told me every day how much they loved me—my family, my wife, and the confused voice within me.

The longer I stayed in this situation, the more ill, unhappy, and angry I became. I started to become short tempered, my career suffered, and my internal batteries were constantly drained.

One evening, after my mother started to insult me in front of my wife, I couldn't take it anymore. I kissed everyone, told them I was going out to attend to some business, and drove to the mountains of Macedonia. I was ready to commit suicide.

I chose the same place where I had asked the universe to help me be strong and change my sexuality. Under the most amazing, starry night, falling stars, and still nature, I asked the universe to help me be the "normal" guy everyone expected me to be. It was the same place where I had proposed to my wife, the place where I had sworn I would love her, be by her side, and be the best father to our children I could be.

I was ready to face death rather than shame, judgment, my fears, my beloved wife, my family, and the world. That was the moment I experienced something I'd heard happened only in stories or movies. As I stepped into the abyss to plunge to my death, out of nowhere, something invisible took hold of me, I felt being pushed backwards and physically put back on the spot from which I just attempted to jump.

I was confused, shocked, and uncertain of what had just happened. I didn't know if I had fallen asleep crying or if it was something that happened only in the stories I'd been read as a child. All I could remember was that at one moment I was making a step forward to fall to my death and suddenly was back on solid ground. I heard a loud voice.

"You chose this journey. It is not your time. You have a long life ahead of you, a global mission to bring love to the four corners of the world that will inspire millions of people to follow your footsteps and learn the importance of inner peace, acceptance, and speaking their inner truth.

"It's time for you to realize who you are. Listen to your voice, the one that loves, the one that speaks and knows the truth of who you really are. You are a son of light, a powerful Atlantean healer, a master of balance, and an ambassador of peace, love, freedom, and acceptance!"

I couldn't understand what had just happened. Who was the strong man who had caught me almost in midair and saved my life? I caught my breath and turned to find out who this man was, why he had followed me, and why he had saved my life.

But there was no one around. Just pitch darkness and the stars. Just moments before, it had been as bright as day when I was being physically pulled back onto the mountain from falling into the abyss. The brilliant flash of light I had experienced had disappeared just as quickly as it had appeared, and with it went what I could only describe as the guardian angel who had just saved me.

I wasn't drunk. I knew it wasn't just a creation of my imagination. What had just happened was another miracle of God, who had saved me from my abuser years earlier. I remembered the angels God had sent to help me heal my body and survive the minefields that had claimed the lives of many of my comrades.

I kept looking around to find the person, the angel, the savior who had just saved my life. I shouted, "Who are you? Where have you gone? Why did you save me? How can I continue to live knowing what I have to face?" There was total silence. No answer. I felt alone.

I closed my eyes, took few breaths, and meditated. I experienced my body becoming bright, as if someone had turned on a lightbulb in me. I realized that what had just happened only happened with the power of the unseen divine. The same power that had granted my wish to get married was the same power that had just saved my life. I was humbled in the presence of such divine energy, the sparkling stars, God, and his army of angels. I was grateful for everyone and everything that had ever happened to me.

I had known of the existence of angels from a young age and from the many times I'd been unconscious in a hospital bed and ready to cross over into the spirit world. Though I'd had many conversations with angels, until that moment, I had never experienced their physical power.

I sat at the edge of the mountain and cried until the sun started to rise. The sunrise I saw was the same one I experienced in me throughout my meditation. As the sun's rays embraced everything, I stood, went to the car, and drove off. I left the mountain of solitude and returned home ready to face my pain and my fears and everyone I loved and honor the truth I knew inside. My experience helped me summon the courage to face all I had feared all my life.

I told my wife that I was leaving her not because I didn't love her but because of the true love I had for her. She cried a lot. She reassured me that things would get better, that all I had to do was be more patient and trust in God. She said that in time, I would come around and be the straight husband she believed I was.

I knew then that though my being gay was a hard concept for my wife to grasp, I had to speak my truth and walk away from everything we had worked hard for and had sacrificed a lot for.

I told her that being gay wasn't something that would change and that it was time for me to face this truth, all the fears, the threats, the shame, and the guilt and clean up the mess we had created by not being honest with ourselves and with each other's families. I couldn't be the husband she so badly wanted to have and that I was so desperate to be. I refused to live my life in the dark shadows of other people's needs and wants of me.

I told my mother, sisters, and brother the truth. Because of the many judgmental, emotional, and verbal attacks I was subjected to, I left my family home with a decision to never return to surroundings where I wouldn't be accepted or loved for all I was. I had to honor my personal truth and stand up and accept all I was.

I knew I had just left behind everything I loved, cared for, and worked very hard to achieve. But that was the price I had to pay to live authentically, be free to be me, and honor my true voice, the voice that came out of my depths and was ready to play, be free, and express the love and the joy I knew I was. I finally escaped the inner prison I had lived in for many years. I let go others' expectations of me and accepted the man I was. For the first time in my life, I honored my heart's desires with no guilt, fear, or shame.

That was when I truly got to know the power of intentions and beliefs and understood how living up to others' expectations led only to loneliness, frustration, rejection, physical and emotional pain, anger, unhappiness, and feelings of being uncared for and unloved. Through that journey, I learned to accept my truth. In that moment of gratitude, tears of inspiration flowed from my eyes like a fresh waterfall falling from a mountain into the valley called love. That was the first time in my life that I had honored my own values, listened to my inner voice, and decided to speak nothing but the truth.

I learned the art of gratitude and to love and accept myself totally. I freed myself from the perceptions, beliefs, and the mind-set that had kept my inner child feeling unheard, unloved, uncared for, and lonely.

I thank everyone who was part of this emotional roller coaster ride that brought me to a place in myself that is balanced, truthful, and loved, the place from which I now serve humanity. I am because of you. I love you.

BEING REDUNDANT

When I was going through this major identity crisis, I had to face redundancy at the job I had held for over nine years and all the uncertainty that followed. Fear, loneliness, rejection, and feelings of unworthiness took over my entire being and once again stifled my sense of belonging.

What followed brought me to my knees, to a place where I almost lost everything that for the last twenty years I'd worked so hard to achieve. I ended up questioning everything about me as well as the backstabbing games and the façades of many in the corporate world.

The job I had at the time required me to help set up a stable, state-of-the art IT infrastructure that supported my company's vision, mission, and growth. Despite having an exemplary track record and having taken no sick days, one day after I returned from a weekend trip to Paris, I was called in a meeting by HR and my former director I reported to and was told that I faced a disciplinary action. A member of the senior executive team believed I had abused my company's trust. Despite me informing her of the reasons I had to stay in Paris was due to me being ill, she believed that I hadn't been sick while I was in Paris and that I should be disciplined and dismissed for trying to be paid for a day that I did not work. The reason I was told she believed this was the case was that when I called in sick, I had failed to disclose where I was.

This event was the first in a chain of events that made me realize the toxic effects that come from downturns in the economy and working with individuals who foster a distrustful, backstabbing company culture. The people who had entrusted me to look after the company's information systems turned their backs on me in a second. I found out later the many other employees who had been with the company for a very long time faced the same treatment as they were forcefully pushed to resign without a pay or made redundant.

I felt frustrated, disappointed, betrayed, and lonely as I tried to achieve clarity about what was really happening. I had been sick while on holiday, something that happens to many people. I couldn't comprehend how overnight I had gone from being the most trusted employee to being someone escorted by security out of the building. If you've gone through the experience of being accused of something you haven't done, you can imagine the pain, the separation, the loneliness, and the anger I felt.

Based on all the papers, the gossip in the office, and spending cuts, I knew the company was facing financial problems as the market crashed. What I didn't know was the dishonesty that resulted from the company's desire to slash costs at any expense. They had wanted to find any reason to get rid of high-paid employees, including me. They said I had abused the company's trust, but as I dug deeper, I learned the real motive.

I was called into the boardroom and was informed I had been put under disciplinary procedure. They didn't allow me to pick up my belonging until the hearings were finished.

The 2008–09 market crash caused chaos for most businesses. Many people lost their jobs during the crash, but unfortunately, some just like me were victims of circumstances created by the pressure, fear, and uncertainty that came with such a financial meltdown.

That week, I sought the guidance of my spiritual coach John, my healer Martin, and my friend James, a solicitor. At the end of the day, I went home, lit a candle, and meditated. I turned to my higher self, the spirit world, and to God for guidance.

As I completed my meditation, something shifted. I was certain I felt different. The anger that had come from being treated like a criminal for having been ill one day in many years of loyal service disappeared. A dark veil lifted.

I also knew from the conversations I'd had with James that by law I hadn't been required to say where I was when I was sick. My solicitor told me that my company had no grounds to dismiss me the way they had and that most likely if I took them to a tribunal, they would lose and would offer to settle out of court. My heart opened. I had empathy, compassion, and love for the people involved in the false accusation. I knew they had operated from fear, not from a place of love and trust.

That night once again, my prayers were answered. I heard the same angelic voice that had saved my life when I tried to commit suicide.

"Do not worry. Your heart, intentions, and loyal service will prevail. All you have to do is listen, be calm, and present. Let them go through the process. At the last meeting, you will present a document that you have but are not aware of that will reveal the truth.

"Trust your journey and that all will be okay. In the next few days, you will receive higher guidance. You will also see the event that will help you gain the clarity you require to see the game being played. This will equip you with all the information needed for the company to realize its wrongdoing. You will walk away with your name being cleared, a letter of apology, and the redundancy package you are entitled to."

Six weeks passed by quickly. To deal with my anger, fear, and uncertainty, I went to the gym and meditated every day. Each time I meditated, I woke with a sense of inner knowing, peace, and the knowledge all would be okay. I didn't know how that would happen; I just trusted in love and that all I had done for the company would set the record straight.

I attended all the meetings and listened to their arguments, threats, and bullying. It became obvious that their tactics were meant to force me to quit without being paid my notice period and the minimum redundancy required by law.

The day the angelic voice had told me would come did come before my last meeting. I meditated and clearly saw what the executive board was planning and why they were doing it. I knew how many they were doing it to. I knew their motives. I saw me reading a book in which I knew I'd find what I needed to turn the situation around.

I woke up feeling fresh, certain, and clear. I knew that spirits, God, and my nine years of loyal service were on my side and would support me through what in six weeks of investigation had become a game of power, control, and backstabbing.

Before I left home, I grabbed the book I was then reading, *The Amazing Power of Deliberate Intent: Living the Art of Allowing* by Esther and Jerry Hicks, and I made my way to the Pimlico underground station. Books had been my true companions during my underground journeys to and from work. I started to read the book. Between the pages I had opened to was a piece of paper. I picked it up and turned it around.

There it was, the evidence I needed to clear my name and prove I had done nothing wrong. It was a note written by the French doctor who had visited me in the hotel on the day I had been extremely ill and bedridden. Tears of gratitude fell from my eyes. I smiled and thanked God, his army of angels who had once again saved my life, the universe, and everyone else who believed in me. The whole, unnecessary, painful, dishonest process that had left me almost homeless, suicidal, emotionally drained, and helpless due to defamation was coming to a conclusion in my favor.

Though I could have had a lawyer present at all the meetings, I chose to defend myself, stand for what I believed was right, and happily face every meeting alone. I remembered clearly the last meeting with my employers and HR. I walked into the meeting with clarity, compassion, and empathy. In my book, I had the evidence that would prove my innocence and expose their game.

In the meeting, despite the appeal in which I had answered in detail all their questions and had mentioning that by law employees weren't required to tell their employers where they were when they called in sick, they read their decision. They wanted to dismiss me. A member of the executive team claimed with certainty that I had abused the company trust and couldn't be trusted anymore for having used a sick day to prolong my weekend break in Paris.

I remember how calm I was that day as I saw triumph in their eyes. Their egos were inflated, powerful, and threatening. They said I was dismissed with no pay; if I kept quiet, they would give me a reference.

When I was asked if I wanted to say anything, I stood, smiled, and thanked them for all the wonderful years of employment, for the opportunities they had given me, and for helping me through the hard times when my dad passed away. I thanked them for making me aware of their true intentions, the dangerous game they were playing, the backstabbing I had experienced, and their fear-driven decision that had almost destroyed my private and professional life.

I gave each one a photocopy of the doctor's note. I thanked them for listening and for their decision to dismiss me without pay. I told them I would take my case to the industrial tribunal and sue the company for unfair dismissal, defamation, and emotional harm by intent.

There was total silence, a stillness you may have seen in the movie *Matrix*. The HR manager and board members panicked. For the first time in six weeks, I felt they would listen to the truth. This had come so unexpectedly to them; they thought they had the matter of my dismissal well in hand. They knew what games they had been playing with me and other employees. They had ignored my appeal, they had refused to listen to my version of the story, and they clearly had no mercy in their attempt to destroy everything I had built over many years of service.

What happened next was another miracle from God. All the charges against me were instantly dropped, and a formal apology followed. I was asked to get back to my post. I thanked them for their kind offer, the 10 percent salary increase for the inconvenience and emotional harm they had caused during this process. I shared with them an old proverb: "When the glass is broken into pieces, it cannot be fixed. In the same way, when trust is broken, it cannot be fixed."

I thanked them for teaching me a great business lessons in life—to be truthful, compassionate, and aware of toxic environments generated by senior executives who during an economic downturn operated from fear and created long-term toxic effects that could damage a company's reputation for years. I told them I had learned how unhealthy that could be for employers and employees in any business.

As a thank-you for their support when my father passed away, and coming from a place of truth and unconditional love, I offered to take them to court and let the industrial tribunal decide the outcome or simply accept from the company my pay for a notice period and the minimum legal redundancy package I was due.

They instantly agreed. My name was cleared by writing an official letter of apology, and an official e-mail was sent to all employees in the company to apologize for the misunderstanding that had led to my being falsely accused.

I went to my desk, picked up my things, thanked my team members, and send a companywide e-mail informing them of my decision not to work there any longer. I wished them good luck through the uncertain times ahead.

That evening, many work colleagues came to my leaving party, and after a few drinks, many of them shared their personal struggles and the backstabbing they had endured at the hands of their senior managers. They spoke of their fears and experiences. Many shared with me what they truly felt about their jobs and their managers. Most feared they could be next.

I was free of the burden I had carried for six weeks. It reinforced my belief in trusting my journey, speaking my truth, and honoring the infinite wisdom of love and the spirit world that had been guiding me through this adversity.

Leaving the job that I loved turned out to be the greatest blessing. It was the beginning of a chain of events that led me to start on an entrepreneurial journey and changed the direction of my life. After that, I started coaching many people who were going through uncertain times and needed someone to help see them through.

The experience helped me understand how the toxicity I had experienced in the corporate world was simply the reflection of deep-rooted fears and doubts. I learned how people could be easily manipulated during uncertain times. I learned how money had the power to control the decisions people make and the games they play as a result of the lack of money. My experiences have equipped me with the knowledge I've been sharing so far in our journey together.

I came to understand how through fear we can be easily controlled, manipulated, and left powerless. This entire situation was a great mirror for me to reflect and address the same fear that had led me to marry and later to attempt suicide. When our identities and basic survival are threatened, we can fall into a trap in which the need to make money takes over our lives. When we are fearful, others can end up controlling our choices, decisions, and the way we live.

That situation forced me to reflect and reevaluate my life. In the months that followed, I sent out thousands of applications for jobs, but I didn't receive any job offers or even interviews. As time passed, once again, the foundations of my life were shattered. I felt I was back at square one. Fear kept creeping back into my life; my head was full of voices asking me how I would pay my bills. The voices in my head kept reminding me how close I was to losing everything I had worked so hard for over twenty years.

I felt isolated. I was no longer able to join my friends for drinks, go out for dinner, travel, or send money to my family. I felt alone, paralyzed, and rejected by the society to which I had paid twenty years of taxes. I spent all my savings trying to get my personal and professional life back on track. What money I could spare went into finding online programs, having healing sessions, and working with coaches to clarify my vision. Though I had studied and coached many people before, I enrolled to get qualified and obtain my professional coaching diploma at the Animas Coaching Institute.

I had a deeper calling I had to honor—to travel and help people heal, get clear on how to honor their truth and overcome their physical and emotional pain. I learned to trust my journey despite the fear of where my next paycheck would come from.

I had come to realize that the corporate world was not for me, that I was cut out for bigger and better things. I had come into this world to deliver a bigger message, make a greater impact, and realize a bigger vision. Despite the success I had achieved in each of my past jobs, I knew my free soul didn't like the restrictions my jobs had imposed on me. I didn't want to limit my being; I didn't want to be controlled by a desire for monthly paychecks and twenty-five days of annual leave.

I loved inspiring people; I felt alive helping them feel good about themselves and overcome life's adversities. The inner voice that told me this became stronger. I wanted to help people become leaders, driving forces that created and nurtured a fair and collaborative society, culture, and family life.

My internal alarm kept ringing, telling me I needed to do something different and honor what my heart already knew. At that time, I didn't know exactly how I would achieve my heart's desire; I just knew I had to make a change and trust my innate knowledge, the universe, and God. The course of action I took created the life I now love and enjoy.

I love and thank everyone I have met on my journey for being my teachers. They all have constituted a great mirror that helped me reflect and learn from all the adversities I have faced while seeking love, freedom, and connection. They have all helped me harmonize my body, mind, heart, and soul and create the meaningful life I now live and inspire others to attain.

WALKING THE ENTREPRENEURIAL PATH

You know now that the adversity I faced in life revealed to me my greatest gifts. As my hunt for an IT job continued, I became more and more isolated from the life I once had, but again I turned to my friend Marcello, God, angels, Allah, the universe, and any of my close friends who would listen.

Eventually, my prayers were answered. I received an e-mail from an American woman who needed coaching and healing; within a six-month period, she had lost her mum, dad, and cat. She felt alone, physically and emotionally out of balance, and fearful of what was to come. She had inherited a vast amount of wealth, was in a turbulent relationship, and was physically ill. She flew me to her hometown; her healing journey began the moment I arrived.

We spent four hours together daily doing emotional heling therapy, coaching, Reiki, and body-system healing. Six weeks passed very quickly, and through each sessions, she vastly improved her mental, physical, and emotional health. With every breakthrough, she was able to feel the presence of her parents' spirits and would often feel her cat's spirit too.

She got her health and life back; that led to my being asked to help her with business issues that she had neglected while going through six months of bereavement after two years of looking after her very ill parents. She asked me to stay longer with her and help with the business as well as do some coaching and healing for her family and friends who had learned about my work through her.

Six months down the line, I returned to London with clarity. I knew I wanted to do this work globally, be an entrepreneur, coach, healer, and speaker who helped people heal and awaken their soul. I wanted to help others unlock their innate genius and contribute to unleashing human potential in as many countries as possible. I had overcome many life adversities; I realized how circumstances had put me on a path to become an author, a speaker, master healer, teacher, and coach, but I also started seeing the amazing transformational results my clients were having.

I knew that people trusted me; I became great at helping people see through their life problems and leaving them feeling content. People told me they felt inspired and good about themselves by just being in my presence. Sharing, talking, and meditating together made them feel they were being heard.

This made me acknowledge the fact that I was excellent at it. I had already coached, managed, and developed so many teams in the corporate world. I smiled as I had an epiphany; I realized that just as I was able to fix broken computers and networks, I was able to do the same with people. I was a fixer, a problem solver, a teacher, and a heart-centered healer people trusted and could tell their greatest life secrets to.

I studied in more depth different styles of coaching including leadership coaching, business coaching, and life coaching. I also studied NLP, CBT and received qualification in various healing techniques that my heart was calling me to learn. Every life adversity presented me with an opportunity to learn a lesson and gather more knowledge and life skills people needed. I started to use all I had learned to inspire people from all occupations to find the right career, create the business that was aligned to their true being, and become better leaders of their lives. Clients would approach me to help them find their ideal partner, deal with loneliness and rejection, and find acceptance and true love in themselves.

I let go of the fear that had kept me stuck in the rat race and the disempowered beliefs that stopped me from living the life I wanted to escape. I overcame the fear that kept my greatness hiding behind a paycheck. I took action daily. I learned even more the importance of the power I unleashed when I listened to my true voice tell me why I had been put on this planet and what I was here to accomplish. My inner alarm awakened me to my personal greatness.

During this process, I achieved the clarity I needed to align my life with my soul's true purpose. I started my entrepreneurial journey and established my coaching and healing practice with a mission to educate and inspire people globally. I realized the mountain of value I was sitting on and how by sharing my story I could inspire people to turn life's adversities into blessings.

I knew I was ready to teach worldwide what had taken me forty years to learn and contribute to raising consciousness on a planetary level. I would do my part to change the world by making those changes in myself and letting my inner light shine for those who are ready to walk the path to greatness.

I founded the Velvet Journey and HealOneSelf, and I created the TJS Evolutionary Method, the "alarm" I had developed through thirty years of personal experience, heartfelt research, studying, and accruing phenomenal knowledge and establishing with this an easy path to healing.

This simple, five-step, but powerful method is a unique formula I created through integrating years of wisdom accumulated through my inner journey, self-reflection, and reassessment of the importance the power that comes from knowing and honoring my highest values as well as the truth. In a nutshell, the main message of this powerful methodology boils down to one, yet powerful statement-acknowledging love creates the result that leads to miracles in your life.

The more people I helped acknowledge the healing power of love, the more I became the spiritual teacher, healer, and educator my grandfather had told me I would become. I helped people get to the root causes of their issues, acknowledge the lies that have become their truths, and help them establish safe pathways to open and awaken their genius. Through self-reflection and quality questions, they started to see through their problems, behaviors, thought patterns, and disempowering beliefs. The more I did that, the more they overcome loneliness, liberated their souls, and started to live meaningful lives.

I became thirstier to spread my wings and help more people. I started providing answers and practical solutions to people's questions and life challenges in talks, workshops, one-on-one coaching, master groups, retreats, articles, and on radio and TV interviews.

Most of my clients started to call me Life Navigator, Dr. Love and the See-Through Coach. I developed the ability to see through people's façades, issues, and disempowering beliefs that kept them fearful, small, and unfulfilled.

Many of my clients immediately experienced shifts in their consciousness, achieved equilibrium, and gained greater control of their bodies, minds, souls, and hearts. They started to purposefully move forward and become more mindful and present.

A few years later, my path crossed with Dr. John Demartini. I attended numerous evening talks John held on different topics. Everything he said was a healing balm for my wounds I had received by trying to be something I wasn't. What John shared in his talks resonated with me; he was speaking the voice I had once buried deep in the ocean of my subconscious.

I decided to attend his weekend Breakthrough Experience to help me dissolve the emotional ties I had with my bereaved mother. Because of the close relationship I had with my mother, deep down I resented her; I felt disempowered, controlled, and manipulated. It dictated the decisions I made that had led me to live a life of lies, fears, and deceptions.

During the weekend I did the Demartini Process on my mother, I identified all the emotions that kept me in darkness, discord, and weakness. I saw how my thoughts came from seeing life not as a whole but from the one-sided perception that kept me unconsciously feeling resentful toward my mother, who had rejected me due to my sexuality. Two long days doing the Demartini on my mother helped me leave the Breakthrough Experience feeling free, having deep gratitude for my mother, and even more determined to be the sunshine that shined even brighter.

What I have shared so far is not about my personal story; it's about assisting you to see life through a new pair of lenses. You can also learn how fear, shame, guilt, resentment, and other such feelings are part of the same coin; trust, freedom, commination, acceptance, and love are on the other side. If you choose, you can turn all your adversities into blessings and harness the power unleashed when your heart is free to love and be. Your soul knows this already; it's your lower animal mind that conceals the truth of your soul.

Disowned parts of yourself are hidden from your conscious awareness; that's why I saw many coaches and healers and worked with spiritual teachers. They all became my mirrors in whom I could reflect and learn to harness pain, loneliness, and fear and ascend from the darkness of my shadows into the greatness of my light. You can do this as well.

The Breakthrough Experience with Dr. Demartini dissolved the volatile emotions that prevented me from seeing the illusions manifested in my life that kept me imprisoned in a jail of my own creation. I walked away from the Breakthrough Experience loving unconditionally my mother, family, and anyone who had ever caused me harm or pain. I felt free, inspired, and humbled.

My teachers, coaches, and others have inspired me and been part of my journey. They include Barbara Brennan, Deepak Chopra, Martin Brofman, Nick Bolton, Tony Robbins, Richard Branson, Daniel Priestley, Mindy Gibbins-Klein, Louise Hay, Oprah, Eckhart Tolle, Waldo Vieira, John of God, and Dr. John Demartini. The work of these world-famous entrepreneurs, teachers and coaches inspired me to find in myself the missing code that helped me unlock and awaken me to my infinite potential and the mountain of value I was sitting on.

When people feel abandoned and rejected, they find it hard to see this with clarity. They unconsciously create habits, beliefs, and façades to protect them. These defense mechanisms give birth to fear, rejection, pain, and feeling lonely, uncared for, and unloved. But their inner voices will ultimately start talking to them. These voices were once someone else's, but in time, they become the dominant voices.

Have you ever noticed how much easier it is for you to make changes in your life when you're supported and aren't made to feel wronged, judged, or unsafe? As scientists tells us, our experiences tell us, and life itself tells us, changes that affect our whole way of life can be hard for us to make if we don't know how and don't understand the hidden laws that govern our universe and life itself.

Sometimes when you try to make drastic changes, your built-in alarm will go off and put your survival instincts into action. I created the TJS Evolutionary Method: the ALARM, described in my book *A Path to Wisdom* with one purpose in mind: to help you go on an inner journey to discover within the pathways that will free your soul. I want to help you learn to listen to your unique, authentic voice that may have been put on "snooze" for many years.

A part of your brain that helps you survive sees adversity as a life-or-death situation; it triggers a chain of hormonal reactions. When you face threatening situations, you go into the fight-or-flight mode as you are led to believe you're threatened.

Aloneness is not just an individual experience; it's a worldwide phenomenon, yet we all experience it in a most intimate way. When we feel uncertain about ourselves, that can trigger a whole chain of behaviors supported by subconscious beliefs. When we feel insecure and unsafe, it affects our entire being and makes it difficult for us to change.

Tony Robbins teaches the six human needs. Certainty is one of them; if you're interested in learning more, explore his work on human needs; he explains why they are essential to us.

The problem is that from an early age, our beliefs are created from the environment we were born into, and they end up running like a computer program in our subconscious minds. At a very young age, we learn about how the world works from our parents' beliefs and cultural and religious doctrines. In time, other people's beliefs and values become deeply engrained in our subconscious minds and we end up creating façades that conceal our truth. These masks hide from us the most precious gifts we have—the gift of life, the gift of the creator.

Other people's certainty becomes yours, and you forget about your inner power that knows its certainty. You start basing your decisions and life choices on the information given to you by others early on. At age six or so, you switch from using mostly your right brain to learn to using your logical left brain predominately. The good news is that you can learn to develop both parts of your brain so you can access all your mental faculties to help you in your entrepreneurial journey in the same way it helped me.

I am grateful for your time and patience with this chapter. You may be already reflecting on your hardships and learning about the façades you have built up that hide your true essence. You may have discovered truths that are other people's lies. You can unravel illusions you've created about a reality in which you feel pain, fear, shame, guilt, and other negative feelings; you can change this.

If you're at a place in your life that you wish others to experience your joy in a certain area of life, you may want to reconsider all you know, reflect, and see why and from which part of your being this need is being generated.

You're reading this book of your own free will; everyone exercises free will. We all make decisions through free will. We all participate in cocreating our reality and the universe. Knowing this simple yet universal law, it's an important part of your journey to learn to let go of the illusion that to love someone is to help someone without ever asking the person you love and trying to help them give their consent. When you understand the importance of honoring your own free will, you will honor every human being's free will. The more you do that, the more you will free your soul and honor the greatness of everyone you meet.

Your personal situations may have arisen from a place of separation, feeling lonely, or from intruding on other people's freedom. See with clarity all your life situations that have been fueled by your ego. Acknowledging them with your truth and from a place of grace will open your heart to empathy and unconditional love.

If you get emotionally charged on someone else's behavior, thoughts, or emotional state, use that to help you recognize those disowned parts in you that others are showing you in that situation. As you start to own your disowned parts, you will stop judging yourself and others. You will become better at listening to your voice and to what other people are communicating to you. It's your choice to search within for answers to your life problems.

You're about to learn more about how I broke through my loneliness and started helping others learn to navigate the ocean of life adversities and achieve the paradise of inspired living. Learn how to find the switch that activates your true light. In the chapters to come, you'll partake in a treasure hunt for the true source of solitude. You will learn why just as a computer virus can paralyze computer networks, loneliness can infect the global consciousness and impact us all.

I hope what you have read so far has inspired you to become more curious about how to go further on your personal journey of self-reflection and embody the lessons you learn along the way. Your true essence will acknowledge what you're being shown, and you will start to see adversity as opportunities that can help you expand your awareness of your true self. The more you do that, the more you will start to experience the magic, the love, and the oneness that life is. This way of graceful living gives birth to the miracles you may wish to bring about in your life.

Many ancient traditions, healers, and modern science agree that answers to life's greatest question are found in the quantum world. What they all mean is that we should go within and observe with curious eyes the hidden order that exists at the subatomic level and how the behaviors of the quantum world govern life, the universe, and you.

It is within your power to discover what's important to you, why you're here, and why you feel separated despite knowing the interconnectedness of all life. You will learn that at quantum level, you too are connected with the divine matrix of life.

What stops many of you from seeing this hidden order and how interconnected you are within is the lack of awareness of the inner working of your body and the fears and the habits you have created since birth. It's the framework by which most of you live your life, the education you were subjected to that makes you more logical in your approach and disregard the most powerful element in the way you cocreate reality through your feelings.

The truth is buried deep down in us all; every cell of our bodies holds tremendous intelligence. Whether we acknowledge it or not, most people spend considerable time searching for something to quench their thirst for the truth and the way to express the highest version of themselves. It can become our purpose in life; it can be what gets us up every morning and makes us do what we do.

Your purpose is to learn the truth innate in you, the truth that was embedded in your DNA and in your body, mind, heart, and soul.

BREAKING THROUGH LONELINESS

What helped me most in my journey through loneliness was increasing my knowledge of the importance values played in my daily choices. I didn't know that not honoring my true values would lead me to all the adversities I had faced.

This unawareness of the power that values play in your life can take you to places within yourself that are dark, cold, and lonely. We all see, hear, touch, act, and communicate according to our unique set of values. When those values match other's values, we see with the same eyes. If we pay attention in life, we will see how when we communicate through others' values, they become all ears, they engage with us, and they may become infatuated with us. They will listen to and truly hear us.

In my research to gain a better understanding of this, I studied axiology, the science of value. *Axiology* comes from two Greek roots—*axios*, which means "worth" or "value," and *logos*, which means "logic" or "theory." Thus, axiology is the theory of value. Rapid developments in science have made it possible to measure value as accurately as a thermometer measures heat.

I learned I wasn't alone in this quest for understanding the science of value; this quest originated with early Greek philosophers, and it culminated in the work of Dr. Robert S. Hartman, who dedicated his life to creating a mathematical system that successfully orders the values of our everyday experiences.

Axiology helped me gain knowledge about the everyday world and created a frame of reference that gave me a new way of looking at myself and my environment. What helped me better understand this complex process was reading Dr. John Demartini's books *The Values Factor: The Secret to Creating an Inspired and Fulfilling Life* and *Inspired Destiny*.

The more I immersed myself in the wisdom John shared in his books, the more light shined on my own findings and the truths I had gathered through life. If you've ever heard someone else speaking your thoughts, feeling your emotions, or coming up with the same phrases in the same moment, you'll know what I'm talking about. When I met John, I felt I had met another version of me, one that was there to guide me to the gateways that led to light and the richness of life.

I immersed myself in studying axiology and John's work. I learned how when our personal values clash with other people's values, we react by disconnecting; we stop listening and immediately judge them. We put people in boxes and lose interest in what they have to say. We shut down like a computer. We become arrogant, controlling, and adopt a know-it-all attitude.

As I reflected on my own behavior and all the people who crossed my path, I realized how everyone I met and I were constantly projecting and communicating through our unique values. It was a moment of clarity that changed me and the way I now observe the world. I use it now to help many clients go through this process and rid themselves of burdens that come from conflicting values.

Not knowing our personal values leads us to not honoring our true selves and damaging relationships we may have worked very hard to nurture. Marriages, relationships, and friendships break down because of this conflict in values. Businesses lose billions each year by not knowing or communicating to their employees their unique values.

When you lack clarity of your unique set of values, you close the doors to opportunities in life and say hello to the isolation and separation that the breakdown of communication creates. It paves the way to rock bottom; you fall into the deepest parts of the cave where darkness, fear, and loneliness are your only companions.

Being separated and disconnected becomes your way of being. You lose sight of your ability to relate, reflect, and communicate lovingly. I lived such a life for many years; I subordinated myself to the people whose values I had been taught from early on. In everything I was doing, I put others first; that was what I had been taught love was.

We must get to a place where we realize our separation is a journey of its own we all undertake; it takes us down the path to wretched solitude or brings us to a more connected self that honors our highest values. On this journey, we can begin to listen to our own authentic voices, the voices that know, and the voices that come from the depths of our souls. But we have to learn the difference between our voices and those that come from others' values, those that have been forced on us through cultural conditioning, media, and every experience we have ever had.

The authentic voice I'm talking about surfaces in our conscious beings once we quiet our minds and learn to master our emotions; then we can hear it clearly and loudly. This authentic voice resides in your heart; once you listen to it for the first time, you will never shut it down. As I learned to listen to my body's alarms, acknowledge them, and act on them, I started to hear my soul's call for love.

I wrote of this voice in my first book; it started getting louder and stronger, and it became my guide. It helped me align my life with the essence of my true being. This call for love is the voice our soul is broadcasting for us to listen to. By following this inner voice, committing to the process, and listening to it, I broke through my loneliness. I created the freedom, the love, and the connection I now radiate like a beacon of light.

We are called to unveil and unleash our inner light so billions of others can unleash their light. For this to happen, all human beings at some point will have to go through the inner revolution required for the self to manifest. Some of us in this life will get to know and honor ourselves and our values, listen to our unique voices, and embrace our infinite natures.

The more you learn to listen to your inner voice and learn about your values, the more you will purify your being and honor your soul's calling. The more you do this, the better you will become at accepting others' choices and be free and at peace with yourself. You will see life with the eyes of a curious child, and life will reward you with freedom, connection, and the power that lies in the embrace of unconditional love.

In all you do, respect your free will and see how easily it is to honor it in other people without judgment. This way of being will unload the weight you have been carrying all your life, and for the first time, you will give yourself permission to fly and be the free angel of love that deep down you know you are.

As you will read in the next chapter, once I reached this place within myself, I knew I was ready to teach, resolve global problems, and be of the best service to humanity.

I hope you'll do the exercises in this book and apply the knowledge, wisdom, and energy woven into each word. You will feel more connected within and be ready to be of service to humanity. You will see life as a gift for everyone around you as well as yourself.

IN SERVICE TO HUMANITY

Allow your inner child to be curious about what this and the rest of the chapters in this book will unveil. Your heart is thirsty to discover more about how to integrate your segregated parts and how by so doing you can tap into the power by which you create the reality you want though gratitude, intentions, and your super-conscious mind.

Stop reading. Close your eyes. Take a few deep breaths. Relax your body and mind. Instruct your higher being to help you create a clear mental picture of the life you want to create and live in. Allow your imagination and curiosity, which are God-given gifts, to take over. Keep this vision in your head long enough. Give it a strong feeling. Do it every day for at least ninety days. Become curious about life, people you meet, situations you're in, and the blessings hidden in every adversity in your life.

You'll see for yourself how in time things will change for you just as they did for me and many others who have mastered the enemies and the allies of all time, our egos, selves, and minds.

Ever since I can remember, I have been curious about certain things. Why me? Why is life is the way it is? Why is this happening to me? Why I was born into a family that doesn't accept me? Why was I sick? Why was I abused? Why did those who told me they loved me never notice my pain, loneliness, and fears that caused me to build façades starting at age three? Why do I and many others have physical, mental, and emotional challenges that sink us to the bottom of a lonely ocean? Why are we on this never-ending, emotional roller coaster called life?

Why I am the way I am? Why do I do what I do? For what purpose, for what reason, and for what meaning? Why does God answer some prayers but not all? If everything we create is to serve our higher purpose, why are we not taught about it early on? What if we too, like the technology we create, are creations of an intelligent designer who has a purpose for us?

I have learned that when adversity hits me, instead of looking outwardly for answers, I go inwardly, and be grateful to the person or the situation that caused the adversity for the lesson I am being shown. I tap into my curious, inner child, go deep within, and search for the answers. I ask myself, what was my contribution to this situation? What am I thinking, feeling, or doing that created the experience? Who am I being in that particular moment in time? What can I learn from that experience?

Dr. John Demartini taught me a simple but powerful exercise. I now write down at least a hundred benefits and a hundred drawbacks for every challenging situation I face. When I did this at his signature seminar, the Breakthrough Experience, I knew exactly why I had come to this wonderful teacher. I did the Demartini Process on my mother, and by the end of the exercise, I felt gratitude and unconditional love for her. I saw with clarity how I had every single trait I thought my mother had but I didn't.

I use this process regularly to help me deal with any life adversity, and I teach people how balancing perceptions can diffuse any emotional charge that may be preventing them from living inspired lives.

John's teachings helped me put the entire life puzzle together and were the glue that held together all the knowledge and wisdom acquired throughout my life and put it into the TJS Evolutionary Method: the ALARM. I learned how from the moment I was born, the healing power of gratitude, acceptance, and unconditional love helped me break through my loneliness.

I thank and love Dr. John Demartini from the bottom of my heart. By staying curious, asking the above questions, and working with so many amazing teachers, healers, and coaches, I am now of service globally to companies and people who need clarity and solutions to everyday challenges.

I have become the See-Through Coach, a spiritual teacher many call Dr. Love, and the life architect that helps people design create, and live the life they deep down always wanted but were afraid to take action to bring it into their experience. I shine brightly and use the healing power of love, gratitude, and truth to help people overcome loneliness and life's adversities. Like the sun's rays that give warmth and life to earth, you too, once you let go your illusions, will radiate pure light and help others in their journeys.

This feeling of becoming the expert, the go-to person to help people find the true sources of their life challenges, their loneliness, and what their spirit-guided mission is was the seed that grew fruit that now nurtures many people. That seed gave birth to my first book, *A Path to Wisdom*, TJS Meditation Solutions: the ALARM, and the eight façades I talk about in *A Path to Excellence: The Manual to Magnificence, Wholeness, and Inspired, Prosperous Living.* This seed became seminars, talks, and private coaching programs. This book, the many opportunities that fortune has put on my path, and many more books to come are all fruit of that seed.

We all have unique seeds we were born to sow and cultivate so they become unique fruit to nurture you and share with the collective consciousness. The seeds I planted got me to a point in my life that I made a real breakthrough. I realized I had so many parts of my parents in me—the provider, the peacemaker, the nurturer, the healer—as well as the authentic me who since I was young believed in freedom, connection, and the healing power of love.

Just like my father, I became an ambassador for education, continuous learning, and knowing the importance of balancing the strong masculine energy with the divine feminine energy in us all. By doing the inner work, we become mirrors for others and become bridge builders who help people move from the old energy to new, conscious energy.

Just like my mother, through my work, I became the giver of nurturing feminine energy that many people require to feel safe, listened to, and supported in their journeys to find their own paths, equilibrium, and authentic voices.

By reaching this place of inner equilibrium, we can become the captains of our lives and the lights of our souls' paths. We can influence the directions our lives take and be ambassadors of light who illuminate the path on which we as a species are taking our planet. By being of service with a heart full of empathy, gratitude, and love, we can move into a brighter future.

I wrote this book and bring this gift of light to you from an inner place of humility and grace. I have meditated and listened to that call for love mentioned before so I can access in me what you are reading, my gift, light, and love to you from you.

You cannot become a master sailor on calm seas; you cannot be a leader of your life unless you face life's adversities head-on. That's what I did with all the adversities that came my way; that's what inspired me to listen to my heart's authentic voice and follow my entrepreneurial journey, become a coach, and write this book that can transmute your essence, the way you see yourself, and the way you see the world.

When you go head-on with life's challenges, you will start to break through the concrete walls of fear, shame, and guilt and the limitations of your lower mind. With each fear wall you break through, you will reach the inner awareness you need to live in a switched-on state in which you will care about and love others and be at peace with your inner being and others.

Many people live in a fantasyland; they think such a breakthrough will lead them to everlasting happiness. But no human being can create eternal happiness. That's an illusion created by those who like to control others. By observing nature and the duality of life, you'll learn that adversity and positive life experiences will always be present in life; they are the two faces of the same coin.

You cannot become an excellent driver who can navigate by your emotional guidance system successfully without experiencing adversity. You cannot learn to be in a switched-on state without knowing what causes you to switch off, be in the dark, and not make the choice to change.

As I reflected upon all my life's experiences and those of my family, friends, colleagues I used to work with, and the many people who have entrusted me to assist them in overcoming adversity, I reached an unexpected conclusion. Whether we acknowledge it or not, we all have to deal with misfortune and feeling isolated, lonely, and most of all disconnected from our true being, the power of love, and our infinite self, the soul.

I have overcome many illnesses and now help others do the same; I have equipped myself with the knowledge, experience, and the wisdom I need to help people uncover the eight façades of segregation I talk about in A Path to Excellence: *The Manual to Magnificence, Wholeness, and Inspired Prosperous Living.* By removing these layers, you will give yourself permission to heal your body, mind, and heart and reconnect with your essence.

It gives me a great joy to be of service to you by sharing the lightbulb moments you have read so far, the lessons I have learned, and the wisdom I have gained throughout this journey to help you see your world through new, conscious lenses.

If you feel alone and disconnected, allow yourself the gift of the imagination and create an illusion in your mind in which you feel interconnected with the divine matrix of life. Give yourself permission to connect to the magic that life is and to the mental faculties that bring you from a place of separation to a place of connectedness.

The best thing you can do for yourself right now is to get clarity on the reality you're living and the illusions you're creating that may not be honoring your truth. Give yourself the gift of learning, clarity, focus, and freedom you're yearning to have. If you don't know how to get there, hire a good coach or mentor or work with a healer or other specialist who resonates with your entire being to help guide you through the process.

Your integrating and embodying all the knowledge, experiences, and the lessons shared so far in our journey together will create visible shifts in your being and your heart will open up and feel connected to all that is. Every experience shared helps you integrate the knowledge required for you to let go of the need to intrude on other people's experiences without being asked. The more you let go of the need to intrude, the less you will give in to your ego's need to control others and the more you will be present, accepting, free, at peace with yourself, and connected with all life.

Reflect on what you have learned so far; write down your personal life story or tap it into your computer. Go as far back as you can remember and up to today. Once you've completed your journal, do the following exercises and write down your answers in your journal.

- When you're challenged, what's your first reaction? Do you reflect on or reject what you're hearing and focus on a solution?

- Do you completely accept that you are the creator of your own reality, or do you keep searching for answers that fit in with other people's values?

- Are you feeling happy and joyful by silently living your own truth without forcing it on others?

- Highlight the life situations that caused you to feel separation, loneliness, and rejection.

- List all the life situations and people who made you feel alone, separated, and disconnected in a social environment, in a relationship, at work, or with your family.

- Next to that list, write at least forty negative things that impacted you most as well as an equal number of benefits and lessons you learned for each of the negative things you wrote down.

- Count your blessings and write them down. Seek the blessings you have derived from adversity. If you can't find at least twelve for each, you're not digging deep enough. Go within and search for at least twelve blessings. If you're doing this properly, you'll have at least 400 things on your list. Remember: if you don't keep digging, you may never discover the diamond buried deep in you.

If you have completed the above exercises, you're ready to continue to the next part of our journey together. In the following chapters, your soul will become thirsty to learn even more about inner loneliness. You will learn how you too can overcome loneliness, rejection, and pain and reclaim your power. You'll develop personal insights upon reflection of my journey of breaking through loneliness and will apply the principles you derive to your personal circumstances. You will create a lasting solution for the many life issues you face.

It doesn't matter if you feel lonely or not; at this point in our journey, you may not realize it. But to start reversing the damage that loneliness has caused you and everyone you come in contact with on a cellular level, you have to acknowledge what loneliness is.

Learn about your seeds that grow to be weeds in your garden of life and their true source. Become aware of how they spread through society, and listen to the alerts that come from your inner alarm to stop the virus of the modern age called #Loneliness. In this journey together you come to acknowledge the impact this has on the way you think, feel, and behave and learn how to immunize yourself against loneliness and other life adversities.

In our next journey, you will become aware of the true impact loneliness has on your mental, emotional, and physical well-being and how it affects your career, relationships, and social and spiritual lives. More important, you'll realize how loneliness is associated with a variety of mental and physical diseases that can shorten your life.

CHAPTER 2

SOURCE OF WRETCHED SOLITUDE

Carl Jung said, "Loneliness does not come from having no people around you but from being unable to communicate the things that seem important to you." If you think deeply about this accurate statement, you'll acknowledge that at some point in your life, you have been in a roomful of people but still felt lonely. You found it hard to fit in and communicate what was important to you.

My aim in this chapter is to help you demystify the true source of the loneliness and the inner discord you might be experiencing that prevents you from being your truth. You will find out if it's something intrinsic or extrinsic. Were you born with it, or did you develop it from life's experiences, people around you, and the billions of bits of information you're bombarded by every day?

I always wondered if the first memories we have don't contain the qualms of feeling frustrated and irked while alone and if those qualms grow on us over time the more we socialize. Does loneliness come from within, or is it planted in us from outside?

Loneliness has many different sources and causes, and it affects people differently. People often feel lonely because of their circumstances, but sometimes, loneliness is a deeper, more-constant feeling that lives in people and differs greatly from one to another.

You might feel unable to like yourself or be liked by others. You may lack self-confidence, self-worth, and self-love. That comes from various sources; one could be from having been unloved as a child. As an adult, you might continue to feel unlovable in all relationships. Sometimes consciously or unconsciously, you may isolate yourself from relationships because you're afraid of being hurt, rejected, or lonely.

I believe that loneliness is a side effect of a much deeper problem—an unbalanced mind that perceives a loss of contact with our true essence. The ego rises when we unconsciously switch on the security barriers to protect our essence. This purposeful, built-in security wall comes up in us throughout our lives to protect us from the dangers in our world.

If you experience deep, unexplainable loneliness, you might spend a lot of time in solitude or socializing with other people in order to fight the feeling. You might react in the opposite way, hiding away on your own so you don't have to face a world of people you feel unconnected to. You may also develop unhelpful habits such as using alcohol or drugs to escape your feelings of loneliness or to help you face social situations you can't avoid.

Western society encourages people to be independent, autonomous, and self-sufficient. Yet recent research in neuroscience tells us that this is actually nearly impossible without the safety of secure and close emotional connections with others. We are much more connected than we are led to believe we need to be.

You are conditioned to think all people are different. You forget that you share 99 percent of your DNA with everyone. That truth is what got you to pick up this book and learn more about the interconnectedness of all life. There is so much more that we all can do to consciously acknowledge the balance in everything that connects us and separates us.

Every life adversity we go through causes pain, fear, rejection, and loneliness. What we focus on is what creates the illusion of being disconnected from the essence of our being. Our focus makes us feel separate, disconnected, and lonely.

Social media platforms such as Facebook have made it easy for billions of people to connect, access, and share trillions of bits of information. Yet the downside is that it has become relatively easy to hide our true natures and our loneliness and avoid the real reasons we cannot connect deeply with one another.

With our present level of consciousness, more than ever before, we need to shape our collective knowing into a cohesive daily practice. Yet we don't do it, and it's for that reason we all must learn to align our lives with our inner worlds and outer environments. One of the most obvious signs of this discord is the feeling of isolation, loneliness, and disconnection we can observe in daily life among everyone we meet.

You can be in a sports stadium with hundreds of thousands of people and feel a sense of solidarity because you're all cheering for the home team, but the moment the game is finished, everyone turns his or her back to one another. You leave the stadium, drive home, and there it is—loneliness.

The Internet culture doesn't allow for the human interaction we need to break through our lonesomeness. In such a technologically connected world, how can we find even one authentic relationship we can trust?

Anyone who has ever been in the middle of an ocean surrounded by an eternity of waves knows how lonely that can be. Outside your physical body, time has no meaning, and distance is just another dream on an empty sea whether you're on a cruise ship, a troop ship, a battleship, or in a canoe. It's all the same in the wider lens of cosmic vision. The ocean in this case is a metaphor for loneliness, separation, and isolation.

I was born in 1969, when the world was Internet free, computer free, and mobile phone free. As technological modernization occurred and proliferated, so did the demands on our time and the expectation we should do more in less time. As more products and services came into existence, our loneliness intensified in every sphere of our lives and in society around the world.

A certain amount of this loneliness is due to greater rates of migration, smaller household sizes, and a larger degree of media consumption. But where did it all start? Answering that is impossible, but I share the perspective I have gained through years of studying science, biology, nature, quantum physics, chemistry, literature, physics, engineering, online articles, and many books I've read and classes I've taken. Loneliness exists because it helped human beings and some of our primate forebears to survive and reproduce. Let's start with reptiles and fish. To reproduce, they lay eggs and in a majority of cases leave them unattended because newborn reptiles and fish are able to fend for themselves right after hatching. They lay enough eggs to allow for losses to predators. This fact is proof of a higher intelligence that we don't see in reptiles and fish that also governs the evolution of life itself. As evolution progressed, animal life became more complex and began exploiting new ecological niches.

These developments had their price; some threatened the survival of the entire species. The young of the new, more-complex species took longer to mature, and it became necessary for parents to take the time to safeguard, feed, and rear their young.

Birds lay eggs, but unlike fish and reptiles, one or both parent birds generally hang around till the eggs hatch and feed the hatchlings until they can manage on their own. Ordinarily, this involves a few weeks of parental time. This behavior can be observed in some primitive tribes who leave toddlers on their own without any parent in sight.

Mammalian offspring require maternal care. The mothers nurture them and in most cases introduce them to at least a few survival skills. The young of small mammals mature rapidly, and like birds, they are typically on their own a few weeks after birth.

On the other hand, large mammals such as lions, horses, and cows take longer to mature, so the period of parental tending is much longer. Still, even that period is quite brief compared with the extended period of parenting required by primates. Human children, chimps, and gorillas take years to reach the age when they can function on their own.

As with other biological characteristics, it seems that loneliness didn't arise from any evolutionary master plan but by choice, chance, and free will. It continues to be with us today because it helped individuals who first experienced it to survive and reproduce.

It's not hard to picture what happened through the evolution of our planet and how this possible source of wretched solitude is just one of the many evolutionary seeds that gave birth to separation, loneliness, and isolation for the purposes of survival.

All types of mammals have brains that create feelings and emotional experiences. Fear, hunger, anger, and sexual desire are perhaps the most universal of these strong feelings they all share, but there are others too. Let's imagine that by chance, a mammal was born with a brain that created mental discomfort every time it was away from others of its kind for a prolonged period. The feeling of loneliness would have prodded the animal to return to the others. Because group living increased the probability that this animal and its offspring would survive, the genetic coding that produced the lonely feeling in the brain was passed on.

Eventually, you can imagine how loneliness through genetic mutation was passed on through evolutionary cycles and became a universal survival feature of the human species and perhaps of most other primate species as well.

With years of caring being required to raise a young human, there is obvious value in having a mate committed to that task and in having other supportive people around. I observed this in my family. My mother would never have been able to have six children and raise us on her own. By the time I was born, my eldest sister was ten and capable of looking after me; so were my grandfather, grandmother, aunts, and other close family members.

Cooperative food gathering and food sharing, group tending of offspring, and group protection against external threats are just a few of the benefits. Evolutionary loneliness was one of nature's ways of inducing our ancestors to find committed mates and form such groups.

In today's fast-paced world, we see an increase in divorce rates, an increase of loneliness in the people going through this process, and the impact it has on their well-being, their children's lives, and their professional lives.

If we zoom out from what our eyes can see and see ourselves from space, we can see how we are invisible; we are specks on a gigantic rock no different from the stones we observe in nature. When we are cold in our way of being, we coexist as separate egos with different shapes and forms. When we are hot, just like lava, we become fluid in nature. In this state of being, we exist as a fusion of the five elements: fire, earth, air, water, and metal.

The air cools down lava, which creates mountains, minerals, and gases. We extract the minerals and stones from the mountains that become lonely, desirable items of jewelry gazing at us from store windows.

In a similar way, when we experience coldness, we give birth to loneliness that conceals our true essence from ourselves and the world.

We go through a process of cooling that buries our inner diamonds deep within us. As we dig deep in ourselves, we find this one-of-a-kind diamond that like a precious stone becomes desirable to many.

A sign of loneliness is that nagging feeling of being discarded, separated, abandoned, and rejected by your inner being. You start to disconnect, tell yourself there's no God, and seek proof about everything in life. You eventually create false beliefs to support your illusions that unconditional love is unattainable. You learn to shut down the life force that keeps you alive—love. You become guarded and closed, and you stop interacting with honesty, trust, and integrity with others.

During one of her visits to the United States, Mother Teresa was asked which was the poorest country she had ever been to. Her answer to the reporter in a very Mother Teresa–like manner was,

> I have been to many countries and seen much poverty and suffering. Everywhere I go people tell me of their hardships and struggles, and ask for help, and I give what I can. But of all the countries I have been to, the poorest one I have been to is America.

Somewhat shocked, the reporter informed Mother Teresa that America was one of the richest countries and questioned how it could be the poorest. "Because," she replied, "America suffers most from the poverty of loneliness."[2]

Just because we strive to achieve financial independence and better education and to wear nice clothes doesn't make us rich. Perhaps the answers lies in the words of Mother Teresa. We attain true wealth by living in a meaningfully connected way, not by measuring ourselves only by the content of our material value.

Her spoken truth about the loneliness she saw in America was verified by a 2006 study in the *American Sociological Review*. This research found that Americans on average had only two close friends in which to confide; that was down from an average of three in 1985. Pause for a few seconds

---

[2] The quote was used with the permission of the Mother Teresa Center, exclusive licensee throughout the world of the Missionaries of Charity for the works of Mother Teresa.

and imagine what that figure might be this moment not just in the United States but also globally. Learning the actual figure of the number of people around the world may be the catalyst we all need to acknowledge the true consequences of loneliness in our personal relationships, health, family, finances, spiritual development, and careers.

We make daily choices and decisions that affect us throughout our lives and in every area of them. Yet the truth is many of us lack the awareness to make choices and decisions that lead to being one with ourselves and help us grow and evolve.

Instead, we allow daily distractions to take control of our choices and we end up giving our power away. We live alone and tell ourselves we're happy to grow old alone. In time, we become bitter, and we ultimately face death regretting that we never really lived. It's is time to wake up, listen to your built-in alarm, awaken to your heart's calling, and honor your truth.

Many of us never revisit the decisions that created the conditions in which the seeds of loneliness grew. The more we ignore our inner truth and the impact those decisions have on our lives, the more lonely seeds we will plant and become a forest that that prevents us from making contact with the outer world, from shining, and from letting our true being be free and radiate love.

In time, you start forgetting the moments, memories, and trauma you created through your choices and decisions. You stop seeing yourself as the cause of your adversities and start blaming others. You lack the clarity to see that the loneliness created through this process tells you that you've disconnected from your truest being.

Through understanding the science of the duality of our nature, we know that at any moment, the world is in equilibrium. For every positive human trait, there is an opposite, negative trait. Equally, for every lonely feeling, there is the positive side to it that maintains the universal law of equilibrium and restores the perceived lost balance.

When your perceptions are out of balance, you create many illusions that become the seeds of loneliness. These illusions come from the apparent absence of love and feelings of disconnectedness. When you experience internal discord, you begin to disconnect and open the door through which loneliness enters your life. When this disconnection has existed for a time, you experience the absence of love, connection, and warmth. Loneliness is a perceived state of disconnect from the true self, the source energy and intelligence that governs the divine matrix of life.

You experience loneliness when you feel there's something wrong with you and the things around you. This feeling gets stronger when there's nothing around you, when you have no support and no sense of belonging, and when you feel you don't fit in with your family, community, society, or even the universe.

A successful entrepreneur sought my help to overcome the deep sadness, life-work imbalances, and loneliness he felt despite being surrounded by people. Through our coaching sessions, he started to demystify all the issues that kept pointing to his loneliness. The deeper we worked, the more we explored the many façades he had developed throughout his life, and the more he started to pay attention to the alarms his inner self were sounding.

At some point in our journey, the penny dropped. He smiled and told me how he had come to the conclusion that his loneliness was simply a by-product of his falsified state of being in which he felt mentally and emotionally disconnected. He reached a place within himself where he felt he couldn't share his pain with anyone because he wasn't listening to his own voice. This rippled into his environment, and he kept attracting people he couldn't trust.

Having broken his inner trust so often, he began to feel he didn't have a foundation; he couldn't feel strong, buoyed, and connected. As he started connecting the dots, listening to his body's alarm, and establishing internal trust, he felt lighter.

The more he saw himself as the source of his troubles, the faster he started to shift his outer reality. He became more at ease with himself and others, he started to establish deeper connections with people, and his loneliness turned into a self-reflective teaching tool that helped him get to the root of his troubles. His problems turned into possibilities, his sadness into success, and the resistance he once had turned into results.

The inner knowing that comes from the feeling you don't have the inner strength signifies the presence of a light you think is missing. It will awaken you to your self-truth. Of course, you can be alone and feel perfectly comfortable with it, but when you require inner resilience and strength and feel you don't have it, loneliness finds a home in you.

Many people travel the world alone and feel fine doing that. You may go out to dinner, take walks, have coffee by yourself, and feel perfectly fine about it, centered, and at peace with yourself. But when something negative happens in your life and you have no one to support you, unknown to your conscious awareness, loneliness creeps back into your life the way night seamlessly appears after daylight goes.

Reaching a calm, spiritual, inner place helps you feel grounded and centered in solitude, but when you are spiritually disconnected, you start to have moments of doubt and feel something is missing in your life. You begin to disconnect from everything you know. You create the void, the darkness, and the isolation that leads you to the cave of wretched solitude.

The distorted perception of your inability to connect with your spirit, the divine higher mind, the supreme being, other people, and nature makes you feel disconnected, rejected, and lonely. This can lead to the denial of the physical contact you may need and crave deeply, and that will cultivate the seeds of loneliness from which negative emotions emerge. You feel rejected, disconnected; you enter the cave of solitude.

Loneliness arises through a lack of personal contact, connection, and interaction. If you're approached by a stranger who asks you for directions, you will feel connected to that person; you will feel you are of service to another person, and you will feel connected to your mental faculties in your attempt to help that person. When that connection is made, an exchange of energy occurs. In a similar way, when you feel connected with your thoughts, emotions, feelings, and heart, you have that awareness of your interconnectedness. That's when you feel alive, connected, and loved regardless of the people around you.

But in the absence of that connected state, you feel stuck, isolated, separated, disconnected, and lonely. You feel you can't create that connection in yourself. You think you must lack that ability to connect to yourself and the world around you.

Some children, for instance, are happy to play alone; perhaps they have imaginary playmates and are perfectly fine with that. What if you knew for certain that children were capable of connecting with actual, nonphysical entities such as angels and spirits in different dimensions? Would you then be judgmental of that experience? Would you wonder how you too could create that experience, or would you immediately deny that could happen?

Some people find it difficult to believe that anything exists in any dimension other than ours. As we go through this journey together, imagine that other dimensions exist and that angels and other spirits exist. From that perspective, children who appear to be playing alone may in fact be playing with angels and spirits and feeling connected, nurtured, loved, and not alone.

In a multidimensional state of connectedness, just like children, we are never really alone; we are connected to the divine matrix of life. Our cell phones are great metaphors for our being unaware of our connections. We don't see the radio waves that connect our phones to billions of users, but we trust they exist. Why don't we trust and believe in the things we don't see? If we could develop our senses to pick up all sorts of information from thin air, what would that mean for us? In answering these questions, we may discover why we don't see we're always switched on and connected.

From this place of awareness, if we look at the reality we imagined earlier, it suddenly becomes one of many possible realities to observe, one in which we are never alone. We can communicate across dimensions and be in the company of angels (souls) and perhaps other higher-intelligence terrestrial beings. When we listen, acknowledge, and embody this knowledge, we're never alone. Just like children, we will feel nurtured, loved, and connected and of the highest service to ourselves and others.

In this higher state of awareness, we serve each other in nonintrusive, noninvading, and noncontrolling ways. We honor each spirit's free will and offer help only when it's requested. This way, we will not violate the universal law of equilibrium, feed our egos, and want to manipulate and control others. In this state of being, we stop using love under the guise of being loving and caring.

When we are self-centered and think about only ourselves, we nurture the seeds of loneliness. When we think of how we can be of service to others from a state of connected awareness, we won't intrude, and we won't feel lonely, isolated, and not good enough to make a contribution.

People have external, cultural expectations ingrained into their consciousness from early on. These externally generated self-images aren't based on their true values, and that can cause feelings of separation. They create façades based on others' ideals, values, and expectations; they falsely believe such values are theirs, and they learn to adopt them as their own without questioning the origin source of this fake self-image.

The lack of self-recognition leads people to feel they're not up to others' standards; they develop poor self-images and lose sight of their ability to connect with others. As a consequence, they undervalue themselves. They compare themselves to others and measure their worthiness by others' standards. When they don't see themselves as equals to others, they disconnect.

We are bombarded by advertising that communicates desires, needs, and feelings we respond to. These ads are effective; we respond emotionally to such ads because they appeal to our emotions. If they didn't, we wouldn't covet what the ads offer; the emotional trigger would be lacking. We take action based on these appeals to our emotions, and when the ads are repeated, over time, we start believing these ads' messages and behave accordingly.

Similarly, loneliness comes from our perceptions of others and from external information we receive from others we relate to or identify with. We can end up believing that others' perspectives are true, and we can end up aspiring to become someone we aren't. As you read in the chapter "My Journey through Loneliness," that's what happened to me until I took back the reins of my life.

The moment you start to imagine you should be a certain way, or should create certain results, or behave in a certain manner, that's when you start imagining something other than what's right here and now. You become delusional and compare yourself with your self-created image based on your expectations and your imagined ideal self-image that may not be yours. That's when you create a disconnect in yourself. You begin to feel isolated, unplugged, and unloved, and that fuels feelings of loneliness. You disconnect from your essence and the place where you're naturally at peace with yourself and connected to all that is. You lose sight of your present now; you become lost and wander into the past or future.

Let's explore further the source and magnitude of loneliness by taking a wild, unscientific guess at the number of people who are feeling lonely; let's imagine 50 percent. That would mean three and a half billion lonely souls wandering earth alone. That's a lot of people longing for contact, connection, and satisfaction in the spiritual, emotional, mental, physical, business, financial, relational, or love realms. Such absence of contact in any of those eight key areas sets in motion a barrage of negative emotions. These missing connections lead to poor health, mental instability, physical trauma, and disease. Loneliness impacts immune systems, stress levels, and genes; it can lead to heart attacks, cancer, and premature deaths. This lack of connection also sends ripples that affect the well-being of friends, family, and work colleagues.

One woman told me that her mother had passed away shortly after her father had after a forty-year marriage. This is the case for many who have been in long-term relationships. After the traumatic event of losing a loved one, we experience profound loss; a deep loneliness surfaces due to the absence of connection and the nurturing, companionship, love, and support we once had.

Many people all around the world are awakening to the toxic effects that one-sided, negative emotions have on their emotional, physical, and mental health. The more we increase our knowledge of the workings of our bodies, minds, hearts, and souls, the more we understand these toxic effects impact our personal well-being and that of everyone we are in contact with. We experience how these toxic effects spread uncontrollably into our environments through what's commonly referred to as the human energy field (HEF).

Naturally, your body's emotional guiding system responds to any stimuli your senses pick up; the way it does is unique to everyone. When you feel lonely, isolated, and disconnected, the stimuli you receive through your five senses set into motion a barrage of chemical reactions in your body that lead to poor health.

This wouldn't be an issue if you were designed in such a way that all this internal processing of emotions happened in isolation without affecting others, but it does affect others. By design, every emotion you experience is transmitted into the environment by the HEF and absorbed by those you are in contact with. You may have been led to believe this doesn't matter. But in the evolution of today's consciousness, when science is bridging spirituality, where you have the power to access the world's information at the touch of a button and learn the inner workings of your body, it does matter.

You can't ignore the truth that exposes your ignorance, careless behaviors, and habits and the knowledge that through HEF you emit thoughts and emotions into the global consciousness impacting everyone around you and causing a ripple effect.

Imagine seven billion people doing this every second of the day, every day of the week, three hundred and sixty-five days a year. That's a lot of people unconsciously infecting others with unwanted emotions. Each one of you is potentially emitting poisonous emotions that have a negative effect on the collective well-being and your working lives, personal relationships, and the planet.

The longer you continue to act in ignorance, the more you will continue to propagate your negative emotions like viruses that spread globally at the speed of light and infect everyone else. Don't be fooled; wherever you go, you take along your worries, stress, heartaches, problems, and self-destructive feelings. While you may have learned to not reveal your thoughts and emotions, unless you awaken from this unconscious way of being, you will continue to infect and pollute others, and the negative emotions you emit or receive through HEF will interfere with your inner emotional guiding system and you will lose the ability to control your emotions. You will lose faith in your ability to change your circumstances and direct the course of your life.

As time passes, you will become toxic, uncontrollable, and stuck in a prison of your own making; you will feel doubtful, lonely, and isolated. Your loneliness will trigger the fears, doubts, and emotions that come from being isolated. You will lose the trust you once had in your innate abilities to break free.

When fear takes over your faith it will keep you in a state of confinement and feeling helpless with no one to turn to. Naturally, you're designed to cope with external threats and survive through your fight-or-flight response mechanism.

Research has shown that with the increase in technological advancements and increased use of social media, friendship and social networks have been declining in previous decades, and we have a big problem on our hands.

There are several estimates and indicators of loneliness. Wikipedia suggest that some research shows that approximately sixty million people in the United States, 20 percent of the population, feel lonely. Another study found that 12 percent of Americans have no one with whom to spend free time or discuss important matters.

Other research suggests that this rate has been increasing. The General Social Survey found that between 1985 and 2004, the number of people the average American discusses important matters with decreased from three to two. The number of people with no one to discuss important matters with seems to be growing at the same rate as the number of people joining social networks.

Through my research, I learned that in developed nations, loneliness has shown the largest increases among two groups: pensioners and people living in low-density outskirts. Pensioners living in peripheral areas are particularly vulnerable, for as they lose the ability to drive, they often become stranded and find it difficult to maintain interpersonal relationships.

According to Wikipedia,[3] the year 2003 was the hottest summer on record in Europe since at least 1540. France was hit especially hard. The heat wave led to health crises in several countries, and combined with drought, it created crop shortfall in parts of southern Europe. Peer-reviewed analysis places the European death toll at more than 70,000.

During the heat wave, temperatures remained at record highs even at night, preventing the usual cooling cycle. The elderly living alone had never faced such extreme heat before and didn't know how to react or were too mentally or physically impaired by the heat to make necessary adaptations for themselves. The elderly with family support or those residing in nursing homes were more likely to have others who could make the adjustments for them. This led to statistically improbable survival rates; the weakest

---

[3]   en.wikipedia.org/wiki/2003_European_heat_wave.

group had fewer deaths than did the more physically fit; most of the heat victims were the elderly not requiring constant medical care or living alone without frequent contact with immediate family.

These tragic event and many others that are happening globally are a wake-up call for us all to reevaluate our behavior, thought patterns, and distractions that are the true source of solitude. They are what prevent us from being aware of the true impact loneliness has globally.

CHAPTER 3

THE HUMAN ENERGY FIELD

Science and quantum physics acknowledges that we are energy beings and that through our HEF, we send out and receive information and absorb energy from our environment. We can now acknowledge how whatever we feel, think, and do has a direct impact on the world around us and the people we come in contact with.

Every thought and emotion you experience is energy that broadcasts information into the environment. Others around you do the same. What frequency you resonate in is what determines the kind of information you receive and transmit.

If you feel lonely, you will notice that you attract more loneliness into your life; if you are happy, you tend to attract happy and upbeat people. It's what the movie *The Secret* talks about and what the law of attraction is all about. It's how the universe communicates to and through you.

Your thoughts create your emotions; together, they become your feelings that help you vibrate at the higher levels of trust, happiness, empathy, serenity, calmness, joy, love, and others that most enlightened people achieve. Some feelings lower your vibration, including rejection, abandonment, loneliness, frustration, anger, suffering, sadness, hate, and others.

During my high school days, I was fascinated by the work of the well-known inventor Nikola Tesla, who well ahead of his time and the knowledge of today's science said, "If you wish to understand the universe, think of energy, frequency and vibration. (Wikiquote, n.d.)" Ever since, it's been my aim to learn more about how, by understanding this simple yet powerful statement, I can assist people unlock their potential. Of course, this also means that learning, understanding, and changing your inner world stops the spread of loneliness, the virus of the modern age. This is why it is essential for you to raise your awareness, knowledge, and capacity to maximize your potential.

As you become aware of your body's internal workings, you will acknowledge that what goes on in your body impacts your inner world and through HEF your outer world as well and affects your balance, connection, joy, and happiness.

Life's adversities teach you many coping mechanisms that make you resilient. You learn to survive and cope, and in a process you are unaware of, you create poisonous effects that come from the judgments you make about those life adversities. These judgments end up lowering your vibration, they find home at the depths of your being, and they eventually imprison you in a prison of your own creation, forcing you to take refuge in the cave of wretched solitude. You continue to unconsciously attract situations and people that you may perceive are the source of your troubles. You repeat the same mistakes and get lost in the maze of your creation.

Through repetition, you create the same beliefs and memories that teach you these unhealthy habits, create addictions, and become the things you despise, resist, and don't want in your life. If you resist fear, you become fearful. If you don't like being controlled, you become controlling. If you don't like loneliness, you become lonesome, and if you don't love yourself, you end up searching, needing, and wanting to be loved.

In today's very demanding world, time is the most precious commodity. Due to time pressures, you're being conditioned to control or be controlled. The irritating feeling that time is running out, that you must do more in the now, fuels your fears, makes you more controlling, and forces you into the cave of solitude.

The good news is that you were created to innovate and change the way you perceive your reality. You're free to choose to look at the world with curious eyes, to honor your infinite abilities to learn, create, and grow, and to integrate the wisdom you collect through life experiences. At this moment, you can choose to see the world from a new point of view through new lenses that will allow you to see through different realties, expand your vision, and give you a laser-sharp focus. Make the choices that can help you go beyond your perceived limits and bring into existence that which currently may live only in your thoughts, desires, and imagination.

What choices are you making that keep you in the cave of solitude? Why do you create a mental prison in which your desire is hidden and locked away? Just the notion of being controlled can have the power to set off uncontrollable, unconscious arguments. Often, you behave this way without even knowing why you're arguing in the first place. When adversity occurs, most of the time, you're not aware of it or thinking about the effects it could have on you and those around you. You can forget your body is designed with the most intelligent tools and in a way that allows you to create and destroy life. As you can imagine, that's a lot of power to handle, a lot of responsibility to have.

It's no wonder that with this innate, God-given power, you were also given the tools and controlling mechanisms you need to control it for your safekeeping as well as that of life itself. You have the ability to handle it with care and put it to use in a way that supports you in your contribution toward the evolution of humanity.

The power and wisdom that is native to everyone also knows when you're being controlled, rejected, and judged. The source intelligence knows if it's being used to support or destroy itself. It simply does what it's designed to do. It responds to a stimulus that can dictate whether it's self-destructive or self-nurturing.

A young lawyer contacted me for coaching and healing work; she wanted help with relationship issues. Our first consultation took place at the Grosvenor Hotel in Victoria at ten o'clock one summer morning. The sun was shining. We greeted each other, walked into the bar area, and sat by the window where even today there is a birdcage with a statue of a bird perched outside the cage.

We ordered coffee and croissants and got out of the way some of the basic coaching formalities. Very quickly, trust between us was established and she became comfortable with sharing her pain, life adversities, and the reasons she sought my help.

As we looked at the bird looking free outside the cage, I smiled and asked her what I could help her with. She said, "I'm watching this bird, how free it is, how it looks at the world, at us, and how it knows it communicates a message even though it's not a live bird. I'm in a relationship with a man I deeply love, but I feel trapped and can't seem to get through to my boyfriend's ego.

"I want him to listen to me and be more engaged emotionally with me and my work, friends, and family. He has the potential to be more successful and the loving man I know deep down he is. I tried everything, but the more I try, the more I feel he's disconnecting. I started to lose him. I know he's cheating on me with another woman."

I patiently listened to her story for almost thirty minutes. At one point, she apologized for talking too much. She asked me if I could help her with all this and if I could tell her if she was chasing a man she could never have.

I smiled, looked lovingly into her eyes, and asked her with a childlike curiosity if she wanted my transparent feedback. She nodded. I said, "From all you have shared, one thing sticks out. You're not listening to what you are saying, feeling, and thinking. At the beginning of this meeting, when we spoke about how the session would be structured, I mentioned that coaching wasn't about my giving you advice or telling you what to do. It was about creating the space in which you can come to your own answers, conclusions, and action steps."

She smiled and once again lovingly apologized.

I asked her, "Do you believe you're a creator of your life and the reality you're trying to change?"

She nodded.

"Knowing that, do you also acknowledge in this very present moment that you create this experience?"

She nodded with a smile and said, "Please continue. I'm listening."

"Our job together is to shine light on how, why, and for what purpose this situation is in your life. I can help you extract from this situation what's fueling the loneliness, rejection, and separation you're experiencing in your intimate relationship. Together, we will get to the cause of why you're manifesting the reality in which you are experiencing this disconnect with your partner and most important within you. Would you like that?"

She smiled and nodded again.

I asked, "Of all the things you have shared so far, your loneliness, wants, needs, the changes you want from your partner, and the relationship you want to create, whose wish is it?"

She looked at me in silence for about a good five minutes. The more she gazed into my eyes, the more the emotions were building up in her. A stream of uncontrollable tears started to flow from her eyes. Eventually, she whispered with the voice of a five-year-old, "It's my wish ... Ever since I was a child, I wanted to be in a loving relationship because my parents always argued. I never seemed to attract the right guy, one with whom I could emotionally connect. I've always attracted men who make me feel lonely and remind me of my father. For the first time, I see why. Thank you for being the mirror in which I could see this.

"In these few hours with you, due to your questions and the love you radiate, I started to acknowledge my ego. I'm seeing how I'm the one who is being controlling and pushing him away through my personal insecurities, control issues, doubts, and fears that radiate through my aura. Deep down, I feel unworthy of love, that no man will ever want to be with me, and that I don't have control of my life."

She realized she was the source of her reality and had come to me for help to change it. Through every coaching session, we tackled every issue one by one; she self-reflected and learned how the source of her issues had originated in her home environment a long time ago. She had seen how her father treated her mother and promised herself never to trust men.

She was living from a place within that was fearful, disempowered, and longing for trustworthy connection. She wasn't looking inwardly for answers to her problems; instead, she turned outward to abdicate responsibility and have someone to blame. Instead of developing inner strength, control, and feeling connected, through HEF, she was radiating that she attracted partners she could potentially control.

We worked together for a year after that initial clarity coaching session; we worked on creating more-empowering beliefs. She reached a place within herself where she was clear about how to make decisions using her own values. She became extremely aware of her old patterns that had created the reality she so desperately wanted to change.

Over time, she committed to daily actions that supported and honored her highest values. We identified thoughts and new habits that supported her newfound self and the relationship she wanted to have in her life.

Two years passed very quickly. What happened was surprising to her, her family, and everyone she knew. She stepped out of her loneliness and her desire to control, change, and fix others.

She left her codependent relationship she had created and felt lonely in, and she started to enjoy being alone. Her newfound confidence, energy and way of being led her to socialize, dine, and travel more alone and feel great about it. In one of her worldwide adventures, she met a wonderful man she connected with; he happened to be from London and had similar cultural roots, values, and outlook on life. A year later, I received a VIP invitation to their wedding with a personal message, "Because of you."

My client was unconscious of how through the HEF she had attracted men and situations that reflected her fears, controlling issues, and behaviors that led her to feeling lonely, isolated, and rejected. She learned that she was the creator of her wretched solitude in which she felt disconnected, frustrated, and alone in the relationship she was in.

You might be experiencing similar issues without being conscious of your role in generating the signal that creates the reality you want to change. The people you're with, the culture you live in, your job, and your environment are mirrors in which you can see how through the HEF you transmit you create your own solitude. The choices you have to make to change the reality you don't want have to come from within and be spread into your outer reality through your HEF.

Many people in your environment could be the source of the HEF that when listened to leads you to the cave of wretched solitude.

CHAPTER 4

LISTEN TO YOUR ALARM

If for argument's sake the family or society you were born into is very narrow minded, religious, controlling, manipulative, and out of touch with the rest of the world, it is natural that you become automatically isolated from the rest of the world.

You will be isolated from the knowledge and wisdom that can come from being exposed to other religions, doctrines, and teachings that can potentially help you learn, grow, and be more. Putting on new lenses that can expand your vision, mission, and your understanding of life requires you to listen to your authentic self. Otherwise, you will adapt to living in isolation, hold on to certain beliefs, and form the habit of never questioning the truth that comes from the environment in which you were born.

At some point, you may travel out of your environment and make contact with people from all walks of life. You may start to bond, get close with others, and share thoughts, ideas, and experiences that will help you learn and grow. The more you do so, the more you will feed your brain new knowledge, beliefs, and wisdom. The bigger the desire to question the unquestionable will become, and the greater the chances you will have to attract people on a similar journey.

The more you learn about others, the more you will learn about parts of yourself you never knew existed. In this process of learning, reflecting, and sharing with others, you will start to question your social, cultural, religious, and personal beliefs, behaviors, and actions that come from that isolated place you once lived in. You will better listen to your own wants and needs and the voice within that knows the importance of freedom of choice, connection, collaborating, and sharing.

This unpolluted voice will connect you to your soul's purpose and mission. Your heart knows this voice; the problem is that it's been polluted by years of conditioning you may have undergone in your childhood and later on.

Your soul's calling for love sets off the built-in, spiritual alarm that my first book, *A Path to Wisdom*, deals with. This call comes from the depths of your being and awakens the voice that knows who you are, the same voice that made you to pick up this book.

You use alarms to wake you up, to alert you about fires, and to warn you about intruders. Similarly, your built-in spiritual alarm helps you identify, listen to, and pay attention to your true inner voice that awakens the truth that will set you free from pain, isolation, loneliness, doubt, and fear.

This spiritual alarm isn't something you can see but something you can hear, sense, feel, and know. For good reason, it's hidden in your inner state, the one that knows how to change wretched solitude into an oasis of highly connected and evolved states of living and being. This alarm helps you connect and listen to your authentic voice. It knows how to harness the infinite power you possess. Fear of this infinite power keeps you crumbled in the wretched cave of solitude.

I have observed so many people trying to get to this state of awareness from a place of fear, need, expectation, control, and lack. Unfortunately, coming from that place leads you only back to where you started from— loneliness. You must purify your inner being so you too can reach the inner state of peace from which I now bring this gift to you and the world.

This is a necessary path for you to walk to be able to learn, listen to, and know the difference between your true voice and the one that comes from your conditioning, environment, and people you've encountered in life.

Just as an alarm clock, the sound this interior alarm generates when it rings may be weak, but after a few rings, it will become louder. You can stop it by pressing the snooze button, or it will stop of its own accord until the next cycle.

At times in your life when you feel you are in solitude, you unconsciously want to remain asleep so you don't face the pain of your reality. At such times, your internal alarm can be annoying even though its purpose is to help you take action and listen to that call for love.

Your inner alarm can become distorted among the many voices you have absorbed from everyone around you. You ignore it until a life-threatening situation happens. That will make you listen to your alarm and reflect on and identify the source of your troubles.

Recollect a time when you were physically ill. That was when you had to pay attention to your body and do what was necessary to bring it back to health. You can buy a new car, but you can't buy a new body. You must maintain it and regularly look after it.

The longer you're in this unconscious, disconnected, careless state, the more damage you cause your body, mind, and soul, and this creates more solitude that ripples out from you. If you ignore this inner disharmony, in time, the alarm that is there to keep you alive, healthy, and in control of the power you've had since birth becomes either louder or silent. Depending on your attitude, choice, and decision, you will listen to it or ignore it. The alarm will alert you to take action until you make a decision that will lead you to the cave of wretched solitude or the heavenly oasis of connected, healthy living.

These inner conflicts that once were fueled by the same environment and religion you belong to can support you and drive you to take action to isolate yourself from the toxic effects the conflicts have on your well-being.

Your soul loves the freedom and its infinite nature when it's in its purest form, but with birth, it's subjected to the limitations of the physical dimension, those you were born into. Naturally, it's impossible to contain infinite power in a finite container.

This is the reason you don't like feeling trapped, controlled, and told what to do and with whom. Your spiritual alarm awakens you to these limitations, the control, and the fears that come from within. You awaken to the truth about the power in your limited body and feared by you and everyone around you. Everyone knows they too possess this infinite power; imagine what could be possible if collectively everyone harnessed this power for the greatest good?

This is one of the many reasons why you are told what to do, think, feel, behave, act, and be. This innate infinite power doesn't like to be controlled nor be told how it is harnessed; it drives you to make decisions and choices that disconnect you from your religion, family, relationships, jobs, friendships, and the leader that is in your spirit. You stop walking the path that leads to spiritual growth, fulfillment, and a meaningful and inspired life.

Many people never realize that disconnecting from their true beings fuels the isolation, pain, and separation they feel. The entire body starts to respond to all the stimuli and creates coping mechanisms to deal with the shifts, changes, and emptiness people may experience as a result of this disconnection.

Through an inner, transparent, and reflective journey, you can bring into your conscious awareness the art of true listening to your call for love and dig deep to reach the lonely seeds that are being cultivated.

The deeper you dig, the closer you get to the truth that knows the source of this wretched solitude that came the moment you were born. At that moment, you were unplugged from the source energy, removed from a familiar environment, and sent into contact with a new physical reality. It was the moment your ego was born, when you were cut off from your mother's womb, and your soul entered your new body and for the first time switched off from the divine source we come from.

If you use your mobile phone all day, your battery will wear down and you'll get a warning message about charging the battery. If you don't, your phone will quit working, and you won't be able to call or text anyone or connect to the Internet to check e-mail.

In a similar way, this disconnection from source energy happens to us when we're born. From that moment on, instead of being taught to develop our abilities to remain connected to the divine source energy, we're conditioned and encouraged to stop seeing our always switched-on state and create the perception of being switched-off, feel drained, and act unconsciously. We forget who we were and live unfulfilled lives in fear of being unloved, unaccepted, rejected, and disconnected. We become easily controlled and try to control others.

The fear of being attached to the infinite power, wisdom, and the intelligence that comes from being connected to the source causes us to disconnect from our true selves, the source of infinite power, and the true voice of our infinite, eternal spirits. This perception of a switched-off state creates disconnection, loneliness, and many bad side effects.

The challenge comes when you meet others who aren't protected from their destructive power. You naturally want to help them switch on again, but you may not realize that if you do this without their consent, you break one of the most important laws we all have in common in this physical reality—free will.

If you disobey this universal law, you break it in the name of love, but that creates controlling, codependent relationships. You start to control other people, you justify this by saying you know how connected, energetic, and full of life they truly could be if only they changed themselves.

If you read my first book and learned my TJS Evolutionary Method to overcome life's obstacles, you know the importance of not controlling others. Most likely, you would have let go of this need to control others and freed your soul from attachments that suffocate your being; you would have reconnected with your own truth and gained greater inner control. Many who have gone through this process increased their vision and abilities to see how this was done in such a way that they weren't even conscious of it.

Many of us have been taught from early on to fear and never question God, but this is the same God who gave us our abilities to question and create and destroy life.

The power you possesses creates the fear that stops you from reconnecting to the source energy and live in the beautiful oasis life can be. You adopt beliefs, values, and doctrines that don't necessarily help you evolve. You go on a journey to relearn how to be switched on so you can recharge from an infinite source, help you heal your wounded ego, revitalize, and shine the light you were born to shine.

This happens to most people without their realizing why they were fed lies about who they are, where they came from, what they are here to do, and what happens when they experience what most people fear—death. The fear of death and not knowing the infinite existence of the spirit outside current reality causes them to be conditioned, controlled, and isolated from themselves and others. They become unplugged, drained cell phones that cannot connect to the world.

I had my first near-death experience at a young age. No one could explain to me what had happened. I became aware of this phenomenon later in life when I met scientists and doctors who had studied and researched the subject, which is taught at centers such as the International Academy of Consciousness.

My spiritual quest to find answers to life's greatest questions led me to a remarkable transmedium and spiritual teacher, John of God, in Brazil. I continued to further my vision and expand my spiritual knowledge of what's possible. My calling to learn how to help people heal started in my childhood. Meeting John, an extraordinary man, and being at the Casa Dom Ignacio was part of this call.

A trip to John of God is an experience in which you see thousands of people every day line up to have their emotional and physical issues healed. Scientists cannot rationally explain the miracles that people experience, but I found some of the missing puzzle pieces I was searching for with him. It was where I experienced and found the Christ, the Buddha, Muhammad, and the God in me.

During the eight hours of daily meditation, I experienced the notion of having angel wings, I sensed the spirit guides that had been with me since birth, and I had many out-of-body experiences. I felt I had been transported to other dimensions of reality and shown things I'd never seen before. My life work suddenly made perfect sense; spirits and angels showed me the oasis life could be if I made those choices. I learned what's possible and what I was on earth to do.

I let go of my rational, scientific mind that constantly searched for physical proof and surrendered to life's miracles. I became extremely focused and left behind my personal, wretched solitude that had followed me all my life. I embraced my life work that I now love and do.

What if this lack of awareness of the eternity of your soul was a deception with a purpose? Many people are self-actualizing and are now keen to learn about it. Many are doing something to awaken themselves from the illusion they are living in and are ready to change if they only knew how. Your gut feeling may have led you to read this book so you could shift from your current life to a new reality that is more desirable, fulfilling, and meaningful.

What if the misconceptions you have about yourself, the wretched solitude you are experiencing, and the fears you have are your own creations? Wouldn't you want to know why you're staying trapped in your own prison?

Everything you have learned has shaped your beliefs and values and prompted you to search for answers to reconnect with your true being. The source of your solitude gives birth to your desire to be reconnected and be aware that you can keep in balance your darkness and the light of the infinite power you possess.

Having assisted people globally through workshops, seminars, one-on-one coaching, mentoring, speaking, and energy healing work, I observed a common pattern among people who tell me they are nonbelievers. They call themselves atheists or left brainers and don't believe spirits or anything science cannot explain. But as their awareness increases, they receive a new sense of belonging and knowing that prompts them to pursue their personal truth and its infinite power and its opposite forces that can split you into billions of particles like an exploding supernova.

These shifts of conscious awareness for some of you may happen immediately, but it could take years of personal and spiritual development for others. But the more you develop your unique abilities to access your intuition and the innate knowing of the treasure that lies within, the less time you spend talking about other people.

As your awareness increases, you awaken to new possibilities, truths, and creations that come from this infinite power. You listen attentively to your spiritual alarm that brings to your conscious awareness, and you come to your own conclusion about the person you are outside your body and spiritual self.

Many people consider religion a way of controlling the masses. A good scholar who has accumulated and integrated knowledge knows that religion doesn't control people, that people control religion. The interpretations and perceptions of religion that come from people in a state of disconnect, fear, and lack the awareness of the true nature of the soul cause many people to disconnect from religion. Many world religions for centuries have kept the wisdom in those religious scripts well hidden from the public to preserve them from destruction by certain societies. The wisdom in these scripts wasn't meant to control, divide and spread fear but to support people in their spiritual evolution through peace, love, and connection. It is at this state of awareness that all religion will come together under one umbrella, one voice, and one faith-love.

Your ego and mind can distort the truth, make things up, and delete the information you daily receive and filter through your senses. The truth that is created within is according to the values and the many filters you've programmed your brain to have from birth in the environment you were born into and the family you chose.

Each time I see my clients or others go through this reflective process and learn about and expand their awareness of why they are the way they are, there comes a moment when relief, joy, and connectedness take over their beings. They start to connect to the call for love their souls are trying to make to awaken them to their greatness. Many of you haven't heard that call due to interference caused by the outside, work, and the pollution that comes from forcing your personal values and opinions on others.

If you continue to live the way you currently do, you will remain disconnected from the source energy; in time, you'll be drained of your life force. Feelings of isolation, loneliness, and separation will create a dark, inner prison. You will be swept away by a tornado of negative forces and reach rock bottom. That's where you'll tap into your dark forces that lead you to self-destructive behaviors such as drugs, alcohol, sugar, cigarettes, sex, and other addictions that activate the atomic bomb in you.

You need a place with mobile phone signals to connect to others via a phone. In a similar manner, if you remain in a place of solitude with no signal that connects you to parts of yourself that know the existence of the oasis of life, you'll remain unplugged from your conscious self and stay in an unconscious state of awareness.

That is where you cultivate loneliness, the place that gives birth to all sorts of addictions, health issues, lack of self-worth, financial issues, and relationship problems. It becomes the castle of your unhealthy ego. When you are lonely, you are easily emotionally aroused and driven. You may have been to this place where you felt disconnected and know how difficult it becomes to feel connected with others when all you feel is alone. When you're in this self-loathing, interior place, you can't get through to anyone. Instead, you choose to hide, work long hours, and isolate yourself from the emotions that creep into your life.

The emotions you don't listen to are triggered for a purpose—to awaken you to the danger of continuing to live through unconscious behaviors. Due to this ignorant part of yourself that doesn't listen, you stay in the cave of solitude. These distorted perceptions, lack of connections with self and others, and your fears are the cause of your loneliness.

All right, 'fess up. Go within and search your soul. Here are some questions designed to start you off in the process of listening to your inner alarm. Close your eyes, take a few deep breaths, and ask your inner being to reveal what your alarm is telling you.

- When and under what circumstances have you felt deeply lonely?
- Do you feel lonely now? Describe the territory
- What life would you have if you knew with certainty that you were the creator, the God you worship?
- What would you do if you were the ancestor you talk about and try to connect and communicate with?
- What game would you play if life was your playground in which you choose to become the god you know you are but told you're not?
- Would you deny the wisdom, the creative infinite power, and the love you are?
- Wouldn't you want to create an outlet for all the creative inspiration that comes from this infinite being you know you are?
- Would you enter the cave of solitude to listen to your call for love, or would you simply create the oasis in which you could listen to the symphony of your soul's call for love?

Please take a moment to write out your answers to these questions and see if by listening to your inner alarm you can access the source of your solitude and the source of God that is you and in you.

CHAPTER 5

KNOW THE CAUSE, REVEAL THE EFFECTS

We're in the midst of a loneliness epidemic, the virus of the modern age. You have learned much about the source of this from various life aspects. In this chapter, I will reveal the many causes and the effects that loneliness can have on you and others through the HEF.

Loneliness is a human condition. The existentialist school of thought views loneliness as the essence of being human. Each human being comes into the world alone, travels through life as a separate person, and ultimately dies alone. But you have the innate abilities to cope with this, accept it, and learn how to direct your life.

Some philosophers, such as Sartre, believe epistemic loneliness is a fundamental part of the human condition because of the conflict between our desire to have meaning in life and the nothingness of the universe. Other existentialists argue that human beings actively engage each other and the universe as they communicate and create and that loneliness is merely the feeling of being cut off from this process.

According to research conducted by John Cacioppo,[4] a University of Chicago psychologist and a top loneliness expert, states that loneliness is strongly connected to genetics. Other contributing factors include situational variables such as physical isolation, moving to a new location,

---

[4]   Cacioppo, J. et al. (2008). *Loneliness: Human Nature and the Need for Social Connection*. New York: W. W. Norton.

and divorce. The death of someone significant in a person's life can also lead to feelings of loneliness.

In my experience and that of many I have helped, loneliness can also be attributed to internal factors such as low self-esteem, distrust, fear, and lack of clarity on the workings of the physical body, mind, and heart. It is also a symptom of psychological disorder such as depression and anxiety.

When you lack clarity in your personal values and lack direction and purpose in life, you'll experience internal conflicts that lead you to feeling alone, isolated, and not good enough. People who lack self-confidence believe they're unworthy of the attention or regard of others. This leads to isolation, emotional roller coaster rides, chronic loneliness, and illness.

Another cause of the feeling of loneliness is the lack of intimate relationships. You may know many people and have many friends, but if your relationships with them are superficial, false, and dishonest and you never share your emotions with them, you will feel lonely, unloved, and uncared for.

Sharing your emotions and secrets with people will help you overcome loneliness and help you get closer to the people you want to connect with. In this process, you will disassociate with those with whom you cannot have meaningful, trustworthy, and transparent relationships.

Another cause of loneliness is feeling not listened to or welcomed even when you are with others. If you feel people don't like you, you won't be able to form intimate relationships with them and will end up feeling lonely even in their presence.

So far in our journey together, you may have learned new concepts, reflected on your life's challenges, and see how the way you live gives birth to your unique loneliness. You may wonder if you're in a state of being where you clearly can't see the early symptoms of loneliness. You may wonder how you can move from this path and state of being to one of connection, love, and freedom. You may wonder how you can listen to your body's alarm so you can identify the triggers, the early symptoms, the causes, and the effects.

What you have read so far and may have integrated in your being will help you raise your awareness so you can see the distractions that may lead you to operate in this unconscious state in which you are disconnected from your true powers. You may have learned to switch off your ESP and inbuilt abilities such as intuition, remote viewing, distant healing, psychic abilities, and sixth sense. Through years of conditioning, you may have developed a fear of death without truly seeing, understanding, and knowing the consequences that fear has on your innate ESP abilities.

If you continue thinking in the short-term, you'll naturally stop considering yourself an eternal soul and not invest time and energy in the existential life program of your soul. This short-term thinking affects the eight key areas of your life. If, like me, you worked in or are working in the corporate world, you know how short-term thinking is reflected at you by the fact that most businesses don't have long-term business strategies.

The scary truth is that most of you and companies don't think about the long term impact of your actions. Imagine what would be possible if everyone understood how the current way of being, doing business, creating products, and making decisions will impact the future and generations to follow. What would you and businesses collectively do differently today?

Short-term thinking also affects the way you live daily; your actions impact the past, the present, and the future of your life and the planet. Living in a finite way of thinking, you limit yourself and imprison your soul in the restricted container of your body. In this way of living, you can identify many symptoms of your loneliness.

You continue to search for life's answers, you become dissatisfied with religion, and you live in fear of losing your job. The more fearful you become, the more disappointments you create, and the more disconnected you feel. And the more disconnected you feel, the more frustrated you become with life's challenges.

As you continue in this downward spiral toward self-destruction, you lose faith, become agnostic, and stop believing in anything but what your current reality is telling you. You base your decisions on the information you receive through your five senses. You stop trusting the spirit, you stop listening to your spiritual alarm, and you distrust the intelligence you have by design that can tell you the source of your loneliness and troubles and the disempowered state you may be in. This alarm awakens you from living in an unconscious state in which you uncontrollably feed the loneliness virus and allow it to spread in the collective consciousness.

You have the ability to realize the symptoms your body produces, find the cause, and reveal the effects the loneliness virus has on you and everyone else. Learning to listen to your spiritual alarm and learning to decipher its message will awaken you to the fact something's not right, that you're not living in accordance with your personal values.

Most of you live lives searching for something due to the built-in intelligence that knows when there's something wrong with you. Whatever that is, it needs your attention. The infinite intelligence in you knows there's so much more to life.

There is a greater purpose to life, a greater meaning, and there are answers to your life's questions you can find not just through logic, emotions, and the five senses but also through your sixth sense, the spiritual connection to your higher self, and the source energy we all come from.

Not knowing the difference between aloneness and loneliness causes a huge disconnect within yourself, others, and life. Aloneness is in your nature, but what turns it into loneliness is the many life distractions you have created that make you remain a stranger to yourself. Instead of seeing aloneness as tremendous beauty, bliss, silence, and peace, you see it as loneliness.

When you surrender to the intelligence that created all you experience and give yourself permission to go into your loneliness, you may be surprised that at the very center of loneliness is beautiful aloneness. You learn how loneliness paves the way for you to find the bliss, the stillness, and the peace that lives in the oasis of connected living.

When you realize your beautiful aloneness, you will become a totally different being. If you know your aloneness, even in your loneliness, you won't feel lonely.

As many people have, you too can achieve this state of aloneness through balancing your perceptions, meditation and daily make time to practice mindfulness. It's the best way in my opinion. I created TJS Meditation Solutions to support you in your daily meditation to create that stillness in yourself so you can listen to your alarm and change loneliness into aloneness.

People who know how to be alone know how to meditate easily and effortlessly enter altered states of awareness. As you explore your solitude, you will learn that being your divineness is your personal truth. In this isolation, you will disappear as an ego and find yourself as life itself—deathless and eternal.

By design, you function best when this inbuilt, social need to make contact with others and feel connected is met. It's easier to be motivated and inspired and face life's challenges when you have people you connect with who support your values.

We have taken this deep, inner knowing and used our built-in wisdom and innovative abilities to create technologies that can make it easy for us to interact and create social contacts globally. And yet we lose the human qualities of social connection, touch, and face-to-face interaction that transmit feelings. Surely there has to be more reasons for the causes and the effects of loneliness than that!

Deep within, you know the causes of your loneliness cannot be surmised to the examples that I have shared with you so far and to those you may have gotten to know as a result of our journey together.

The more technologically advanced society becomes, the more likely people seem to become disconnected and isolated and at the same time connect in ways that never before had been possible. The key to this disconnect is to know and acknowledge the choices you make, the beliefs you hold, and the skewed perceptions you cling to as you go through this rapid technological revolution.

What does science tell us about this? I found in my research that while some have assumed the culprit was a dearth of others to remind us to take care of ourselves, new research suggests there's a direct biological link between being lonely and ill health. If you are curious to explore more, you will find plenty of research data at the click of a mouse. But you don't need scientific proof to know that when you're ill and you have a family member or friend visit you, you feel better instantly.

You are a being of an intelligent design built with all you need for social contact and have everything in you necessary to connect with others. We will cease to exist as a species if we don't awaken to our inner wisdom and innate abilities.

Knowing how important social contact is to your survival, let's explore what makes us lonely. What else is at the root of the symptoms that lead us into the cave of wretched solitude? How can being in that lonely, inner place send us on a downward spiral to isolation, bad health, and even premature death?

The effects of loneliness are no different from those of computer viruses that can bring down computer networks. Loneliness isolates you from the interconnected version of you and leads to havoc in all the eight areas of your life. You may feel lonely because of your relationships with others. At other times, loneliness is a much deeper and constant unexplainable feeling that comes from within.

People often feel lonely because they don't have the relationships they need. Poets write about people who feel isolated, invisible, and not understood, and many famous poets who wrote about loneliness experienced it firsthand.

To learn the cause of your loneliness, you must examine everything about you and cultivate relationships that can reflect the parts of you you've disowned. These relationships are often nurturing and empathetic and provide the support you need to understand your loneliness.

Through nurturing and love-infused relationships, you overcome life's adversities that cause loneliness. To achieve the required depth of trustworthy friendships, you have to seek out, acknowledge, and surround yourself with people with whom you feel safe. This creates the safe environment you need to start your personal development journey and dig deep to find the disconnected parts of yourself required to reestablish trust. That will dissolve the loneliness crisis that threatens the modern age.

CHAPTER 6

DUALITY: THE NEST OF SOLITUDE

When you're alone and feeling lonely, rejected, uncared for, and isolated, it's hard to see the positives in your life, the side of your life where you feel connected and loved.

I will share with you an important existential factor that makes it hard for you to identify the skewed perceptions that cause this internal disconnect. What I will share is a fact of life that stops many from overcoming loneliness and adversity.

The most difficult part of your journey to connectedness, love, and living in oneness is becoming aware of your traits, adversities, and habits that may have caused you to disconnect from your essential self. This requires listening to your inner alarm, stopping to live your life on snooze, and discovering your true self. You'll have to recognize the personal and global effects that loneliness has on you and others. As you become a better listener to your internal alarm, you'll unearth the true symptoms of your wretched solitude you may have learned to hide behind the life masks you've created.

Due to the complexity of these façades, the environment in which loneliness thrives varies and changes from the way you're daily being programmed and conditioned. From an early age, you were taught how and what to think, feel, behave, act, and be. You are being controlled, and most of the time, you never question why.

The harsh reality is that many of you end up dealing with the effects of your daily and early childhood programing, past experiences, and fears. The less you listen to your body's alarm, the more difficult it becomes to find the cause of your inner discord and get back to inner harmony.

This late response to your apparent loneliness impacts your health, family relationships, and the way you treat others, and it affects your financial, personal, and professional lives.

To identify the cause and effects of loneliness, you have to look within to find, activate, and use your internal antivirus software just as IT experts use antivirus software to disinfect and protect all the computers they are responsible for. You must identify and quarantine the loneliness virus so it doesn't spread into the global consciousness.

The same intelligence that gets your heart beating, your blood pumping, your lungs breathing, your ears listening, your tongue tasting, and your eyes seeing also knows how to remove the seeds of your wretched solitude and reveal all the effects. It also knows loneliness is a necessary part of your evolutionary process; it serves a unique purpose. The aim here is for you to acknowledge this and learn to transmute loneliness into beautiful aloneness. This will support you and your soul by dissolving the emotional charges that caused the internal discord. The more you do this, the closer you will get to living in the embrace of angelic wings of gratitude.

Use your built-in alarm to warn you about what causes you pain and plants the loneliness seeds. It will make you aware through specific emotions or a deep knowing that something within isn't right. The longer you ignore it, the faster it starts to create the toxic affects you have read about and others you may have experienced.

The same intelligence that knows how to operate every organ in your body also knows how to protect it. It does this by instructing your body to release various chemicals to counteract threats. These chemicals create various reactions to alert you to a problem and make you aware of your disconnection from your essence. Your body's intelligence will let you know when you're out of balance and not in harmony with your body, mind, spirit, heart, and emotions. It'll tell you the reasons for your withdrawal from your body, the people in your life, your society, and the religion to which you were born. This God-given intelligence also lets you know when the work you do isn't meaningful to you, when you resist receiving the things you desire, and when disconnection from certain people, your culture, and even your family is necessary for your evolution.

Due to the lack of the inner workings of your body, most of you during this self-protecting, intelligent response of your body end up losing yourself in the noise of your thoughts and emotions and spend most of your time and energy dealing with them.

In this inner confusion, many of you end up losing your natural ability to switch on your internal antivirus software that can easily identify the symptoms of the inner disharmony that causes loneliness, eliminate its long-term effects, and quarantine the stimuli that come from discord in any of the eight key areas of life.

This inner noise, thought distractions, and lack of knowing how to master your emotions disables your abilities to connect to your true voice, intuition, and inner guidance system that know the solution to your loneliness. Your built-in intelligence, the higher expression of your being, and your soul know the loneliness you experience is just an illusion created by the greatest magician—your subconscious. Your eternal soul knows it's never alone in this infinite universe with infinite possibilities, but your mortal soul has been taught since birth to make decisions based on fear created through manipulation of your worldly existence and your perception of your duality. You stop seeing the bigger picture and fear conquers you; you become shortsighted and forget about your eternal existence and true self.

You make most of your decisions not based on your intuitive self, gut feelings, or heartfelt knowledge but on injected values and fears. The biggest decisions that many of the clients I work with make are fear driven, particularly when the decisions involve financial losses or gains. Though in the short term their decisions make sense, they create pain in the long term.

By having a one-sided view of the world, you limit yourself and create problems that come from seeing the world through the duality of your nature—right and wrong, good and bad, and love and hate. If you were to observe loneliness and life itself from a much bigger perspective, from one of balance, oneness, and love, you will know that your aloneness lives in your loneliness. Life on earth and in the current understanding of the universe exists in perfect balance as a seeming collection of opposites.

Opening your mind and heart to this truth helps you be one with nature, release the resistance, and see it happening in the natural world and in every area of your life.

When you see life through only one side of any person, situation, or idea, you experience only half of that emotion and never acknowledge the equilibrium you have; instead, you're driven by emotions due to your lopsided perception of a unbalanced world.

In all of the following examples of duality there are wondrous, purposeful implications that once understood can help you understand your life better and more so the life mysteries you may be on a quest to unravel. What I'm about to share with you are only concepts; if you can transcend the conceptual and move toward the unifying factor itself, you might be amazed at the breakthroughs you'll make and how you too can get faster at transcending life's obstacles that result in loneliness.

In your life, try to find the unity of the following and see if there's any border between them. They are not in order of importance, but there are a billion more for you to explore on your own. Let's start with the most obvious.

Positive and Negative

These two make the perfect equilibrium, yet we fail to acknowledge that for every elation there is depression, and for every infatuation there is resentment. Even at a microscopic level, we observe this separation; an atom consists of protons, neutrons, and electrons. Until you learn to label something good or bad, all events, situations, and people are neutral because they have both sides in perfect equilibrium.

Day and Night

You observed this duality all your life; it's one of the easiest duality concepts to grasp. You know the day doesn't last forever; you know night comes and another day follows. Imagine how different life would be without this duality. The combining factor is the movement between day and night.

Together, they comprise the twenty-four-hour period we call an earth day. You cannot know the brightness of day without the darkness of night.

Which is more necessary? Your answer to that question will let you know if you're out of balance or in perfect harmony. The combination allows living things to propagate and diversify. Allow the simple, universal truth that life teaches you to sink into your being.

Asleep and Awake

Your day is divided between these two states. Every human being needs both. How could you decide which is more important? Can one state be without the other? Without deep sleep, could you have the energy to be awake? Without being awake, would you ever desire to sleep? Is it possible to sleep all the time or be awake all the time?

These states beautifully complement each other. They need to be in perfect equilibrium for you to overcome loneliness and live in harmony with life. Isn't it hilarious how we devote so much of our attention to the waking state and ignore the fact that deep, restful sleep is life sustaining and renewing?

Having been a homeless teenager on the streets of London helped me grasp this concept. Think about that the next time you wander a mall looking for new pajamas, a comfortable bed, duvet, pillows, sheets, or a new mattress.

Black and White (or Any Color Combination)

In my younger years, I saw most things in the world, life events, and people as black or white, good or bad, love or hate. I found it difficult to see grey or colors when faced with adversity.

You couldn't read this page if the letters were as white as the background and would thus miss what the words on this page were telling you. The contrast is critical to the understanding. Similarly, without contrast in life, you'd be blind to all life and this contrast to life has to offer.

How does this metaphor show up in your life? How does it blind you to life, and how does it serve you? Write down your answers. Notice how in your perception of things in your life, you find this contrast in equilibrium. The hard things you may be going through in life come to your awareness by being in contrast to the easy things.

Complementary Emotions

Mastery is required to handle opposite emotions, but that's a tough concept to grasp; some of you may find it hard to recognize and acknowledge the opposite of any emotion. This is because lifetime conditioning makes you see more positives or more negatives, and that can cause you to react unwisely.

This is the reason you were equipped from birth with the best, built-in emotional guiding system (EGS) imaginable to help you remain in perfect equilibrium whenever lopsided emotions surface. Most of you were not taught things that could enhance your EGS. In fact, you learned things that damaged your EGS.

To illustrate what this means, let's look at fear. To neutralize fear, you must know that the opposite emotion is trust. For sorrow, it's joy. For rejection, it's acceptance, and so on. How would you know what happiness is if not for the times you experienced sadness? Without the opposite emotion, you'd not be able to distinguish between hot and cold, pain and pleasure, love and hatred, and so on. Experiencing life through excessive pain or pleasure causes the greatest diseases the body can suffer.

The opposite emotions aren't your enemy; they are great teachers that can help you master your emotions on your journey to balanced living, love, freedom, and enlightenment.

Male and Female

The seeming opposites of these two energies when brought together can create life. Every time I see a baby I am reminded of how the fusion of these two energies creates the most magical experiences that life teaches us are in us.

This is the living universe at its finest. In this unification of man and woman, a visible miracle happens. This is why masculine and feminine energies are represented in every human being. Due to many factors, some of you have become more of one energy. The other energy feels ignored; it gets lonely, and it responds to the apparent imbalances you have created. It starts to crave for your attention, time, and love.

These imbalances in the masculine and feminine dynamic in us have the destructive power of the same creator power that lives in you.

When this power is out of balance, it takes you on a downward spiral and causes loneliness, rejection, and many other issues you may face in your relationships with yourself, your intimate partner, or the rest of the world.

Past and Future

If you've reflected on your life through exercises in this book, you may observe in your answers that most of the things you wrote about are either from your past or in your future. But where does one end and the other begin? It's that Catch-22 you find yourself in; was it the chicken or the egg first, the water or the earth, or life or death?

Many of you spend much time thinking about the past, people you may have come across, or situations you've experienced. Often, you spend a lot of time talking about past adversities, ex-partners you loved or hated, or jobs you didn't like. And you probably daydream about the new life you want, places you want to visit, people you want to meet, and things you want to do.

Living most of your day in the past or the future can cause a tremendous split in the way you feel about yourself, and this lets loneliness creep back into your life. I notice this common pattern of spending time living in the past or worrying about the future in many of my clients, many people I come across daily, and in the businesses I consult for.

You know it well—your mind loves to dwell, and when you do that, it's often about things in the past or what you want in the future. It's never about being in the present in the oasis called oneness.

The Coast and the Ocean

As I write this paragraph, I'm on the beautiful island of Menorca and business coaching my client Joel. Many of our coaching sessions are done on the beach or walking around the cliffs of Playa de Fornells. After every session, he walks away with the clarity required to see how each business issue he hired me to resolve is a reflection of what's going on in his inner world.

I love seeing him gain many lightbulb moments as I take him on a journey to connect his inner world to the nature we are observing. As we go from resolving one issue to another, his face lights up like the sun following us on each step of this journey.

I helped him see how the sea after sunset goes from being choppy to perfect stillness in which we could see a reflection of the coast. The more issues we addressed, the more he started to acknowledge how the fine line between the coast and the ocean is a perfect mirror and a priceless business teacher.

The more time we spend observing the rock formations, the coast, and the ocean, the more he saw how they work together in perfect harmony to cocreate the experience of the shore and the ocean as an incomprehensible miracle.

We watched the sea and the coast and wondered where one ended and the other began. Do they need each other? If so, for what purpose? Which contains which? What intelligence created this? What life insights and lessons does this line give us?

If you were to observe your life as a coast and an ocean, observe the line between and the feeling of aloneness in this immense space. If you remain long enough in this feeling, you'll realize how loneliness and oneness are like the line that connects the coast and ocean. Let your imagination take over and see how the coast needs the ocean and the ocean needs the coast.

Work and Play

Do you ever wonder who came up with the idea we had to work? Do you ask yourself why you wake up every day, go to work, and do the work you do? Is it just to earn money to pay your bills, play, and go on holidays? Or is it for a much higher purpose, one that can help you use the time you spend working every day to accomplish your life's mission? If you worked all the time, would you feel a sense of accomplishment or would you feel you missed living a meaningful life?

Many of you work for big corporations and are surrounded by thousands of employees, and yet deep down you feel alone. If you truly entered your inner world, looked at your head as a place where all your thoughts were, you'd see the clutter, noise and mess there. You learn how to hide all these thoughts, beliefs, and information and avoid addressing what's truly going on, your true self, and what you truly feel.

If you ignore all that's going on and decide to play, you will feel guilty for playing. But such head games fuel imbalances in the way you perceive your work and play realities; you have the power to force yourself to walk into the cave of wretched solitude.

Stillness and Movement

On your journey to embody these two opposite concepts, you will encounter so many adversities that can cause feelings of separation, confusion, and loneliness. To even attempt to understand reality without these two basic scientific concepts is futile.

The universe acts through these two concepts; pause whatever you're doing right now, calm your thoughts, and watch the natural world around you. There is an underlying stillness apparent in everything you observe, yet movement occurs. If someone asked you if the ground you were standing on was moving, most likely your response would be no, but if you observed the same spot from space, you'd see the entire planet moving.

Movement, or change, accentuates, diversifies, and endlessly recreates. Through your journey from loneliness to oneness, you seek to be still though the reality is that your mind wants you to move. Your mind loves to create distractions. Try to see how far you will go if for instance you always meditated or always moved.

All and Nothing

Every time I had been in a relationship, this "all and nothing" concept would shape the way I would act in that relationship and shake my being when this condition wasn't met. At some point in my quest to find life's answers and truths, I realized it wasn't just me who questioned and wanted all and nothing; during my twenty-five years of personal, professional, and spiritual development, I came to understand it was the question of the ages.

Play around with this concept; see what answers you come up with when you ask, Can all or nothing exist? Are they the same, or are they the polar opposite of matter? Many of you may often spend a lot of time feeling, acting, and making decisions based on this concept.

I see this way of being a lot in relationship dynamics, families, or in businesses. Life has a way of teaching you to see with clarity that inflexibility can leave you with nothing and that most of the times you end up feeling rejected, uncared for, and unloved. Adopting this attitude of all or nothing leaves little room for flexibility, compassion, and growth and will often make you end up alone.

The key here and in all I have shared so far is for you to strive to get as close as possible to attaining the balance of the two and accepting the duality of your nature as part of your essence.

Life and Death

I saved this one for last because most of you aren't fond of talking about death, the end of the experience called life, but this is perhaps the greatest fear to overcome. It is the challenge most of you avoid facing until it's too late. It's the wholeness of the seeming opposites we all face in our existence. Life and death are facts; there can be no living without dying and vice versa. One needs the other logically, emotionally, and physically.

To understand this very important duality in your existence, you have to acknowledge nature as a wonderful teacher. For nature to build new life, it must destroy existing life. We must undergo this existential process that keeps everything in balance.

Consider Mother Nature—the seasons, the changes, the animals, the ecosystem processes that work in perfect harmony. This is one universal law that defies all concepts and philosophies.

It's natural for beings to die and new life to be born. This process is endless. No one really knows how it started, when it started, and when it will end. Earthquakes destroy life and give birth to new life. Wars have destroyed old civilizations and given birth to new ones. Watching a baby coming into this world and experiencing the loss of a loved one are the greatest miracles of life.

We human beings have been born and have died since creation. This life dynamic exists and continues independent of the forms or names or shapes it takes. The key is to find that in yourself right now and abide in it. Take a moment, close your eyes, and quiet your mind. Settle into the space of your own awareness, your "I-am-ness," your presence. Be it, sense it, feel it, and relax in it. What is it? Try to define it. Does it have a name, a color, a sound? Is it something amazingly simple? Find it. This is the whole, the source, infinite love, the absolute. It is you right here, right now.

What I mean by your right here, right now, is not the you as a concept, label, name, occupation, role, or desire. There is no duality in this place of stillness where you find the pure silence—the unity itself, and the witness of all that is. It allows opposites to dance to the music of creation in the whole, the sum of all the seeming parts.

There is only this in this present awareness. Your body will die. Your memories will cease. Your dreams will fade. Your aspirations will be left behind. The whole, the spirit, and the soul will always be there long after you have gone from this material world.

You are the wholeness, the oneness, and the ocean of infinite wisdom you are searching for. Once you understand that in your core, you'll see how life and death are different sides of the same coin. One needs the other, and ultimately, one is the other. There is no more reason to be afraid because that which you really are is eternal. Rest in that. Life will simply happen, so learn to let go and be!

These concepts may have struck a chord with your personal truth, heart, and the way you see life. You may start to see how duality of life creates the space in which loneliness can creep in, and if you ignore this fact that comes from life itself, you will descend into solitude.

Please turn now to your private journal and record your thoughts, feelings, and insights of the moment. What has your reading brought to mind? What are your responses to the questions posed and suggestions given?

CHAPTER 7

LONELINESS IS TOXIC; ITS EFFECTS ARE GLOBAL

Your entire being knows loneliness and other emotions, whether positive or negative, are contagious. At any moment, you're using all the five senses to make sense of what is going on in your world and how to interact with it.

When you are close to someone who is radiant, happy, and full of life, you feel energized, inspired, and good about yourself. If you are with someone who is depressed, angry, and negative, you feel down, drained, and intoxicated by that negativity.

The way you feel in your inner world is always transmitted through your HEF into the outer world, so anyone nearby will absorb the transmitted information. Positive energy will elate you, negative energy will exhaust you, and neutral energy will make you feel balanced, loved, and in peace.

Scientific studies are now supporting what healers, mystics, and ancient sages have known for centuries. Science too now suggests that your feelings play an important role in other people's experiences of life; they can make others lonelier or happier.

With the rise of online social groups, a new kind of loneliness has come about and is spreading like a virus. It's as powerfully contagious in online social groups as it is in real-life situations.

I'm not alone in thinking about how uncontrollable emotions cause infections in other people through the HEF. Cacioppo,[5] the leading psychologist on the subject, suggests that loneliness is contagious. In a ten-year study, researchers examined how loneliness spreads uncontrollably in social networks. The results indicated that people close to someone experiencing loneliness were 52 percent more likely to become lonely.

According to the study,[6] loneliness spreads much like the common cold or a computer virus. While a cold or flu bug might be spread through contact such as a handshake, loneliness too spreads through coming into contact with individuals or groups via negative social interactions.

We all have come across such people who have the power to bring us down, infect us with negativity, and inject their values into us so they can feel superior, feed their egos, and unconsciously control our behavior. Our hearts and our highest expressions of ourselves don't like that.

Lonely people tend to be shy, hostile, anxious, and socially awkward. Lonely people interpret social interactions differently; they see certain behavior in others as a form of rejection.

In this research, more than 5,000 people were asked to complete a loneliness questionnaire, give their medical histories, and receive a physical examination every two to four years over ten years.

Participants listed their friends and relatives, and many of them also took part in the study. By looking at the social networks of the participants and the number of lonely days they experienced each year, researchers were able to see how loneliness spread throughout the groups. The study found that

- people feel lonely for about forty-eight days a year,

- people are about 50 percent more likely to experience loneliness if someone they are directly connected to feels lonely,

- women report experiencing more loneliness, and it was more likely to spread in women's social networks than in men's, and

---

[5]   Cacioppo, J. et al. (2008). *Loneliness: Human Nature and the Need for Social Connection.* New York: W. W. Norton.

[6]   psychology.about.com/od/psychotherapy/a/loneliness-can-be-contagious.htm.

- loneliness is more likely to spread in networks of friends rather than in those of families.

As an energy being, you transmit into the environment everything you experience within through the HEF. Knowing what you have read so far in this book and what the researchers found in the above study, you can easily see how your personal problems can become global problems. It's essential for you to master how to balance your emotions fast so you'll stop spreading one-sided emotions into the world and become the love you want to see in the world.

With additional social contact that you have through harnessing the power of technology and social networks such as Facebook, Instagram, or Twitter, you can see how easy it is for lonely people to spread negativity, take control of your emotions, and influence your state of being. Before you know it, at the speed of light, loneliness and other lopsided emotions propagate through the human consciousness like an uncontrollable computer virus.

In your day-to-day life, many of you feel uncontrollable, unexplainable, and strong emotions. You know that sitting in silence and working on your personal and spiritual development increases your awareness of yourself. The more you increase your vibration, the more you know and acknowledge that loneliness or feeling emotional is no longer just your problem, it's a global problem that cultivates the seeds of illnesses, negative social behavior, addictions, environmental problems, wealth disparities, and discrimination.

Since visiting Cuba, Cambodia, Vietnam, and Kenya a few years ago, I've been thinking about the global visual assault on our daily lives. We seem to have gotten used to ignoring the daily mental rape we are subjected to without being asked. Unconsciously, we are being programmed to behave, look, and act in a certain way.

Why is rape considered a criminal offense but visual assault coming from the forceful advertisements everywhere aren't? Why do we have to deal with the effects on our emotional beings by the billions of pieces of information thrown at us daily without our consent? Why is this rape of our emotional beings not a criminal offense?

This visual assault can make us feel lonely, isolated, not good enough, and in need of validation. We try to change our natural way of being to fit in with social norms, be accepted, and be loved, but we don't realize the norms communicated to us by society condition us to value others' opinions more than our own. Many are awakening to this forceful, global programming and questioning the motives behind this toxic way of living, being, and acting.

We all feel the effects of technological advancements that shape our lives and minds, impact our emotions, and distract us from accessing our true selves, our eternal, spiritual beings. Climb into a famous London black cab or a taxi in any major metropolis these days and you are greeted by a TV screen that come on the moment you shut the door and bombards you with ads. It's become unfashionable to talk to people you share your home, street, and seat with on the bus or to gaze out the window, watch the sunlight on a wall, admire a child's smile, or watch the city breathing.

In less-developed countries, the way people interact is totally different. I visited Cuba in 2008 and spent hours walking the streets of Havana. I felt I was with Michael J. Fox in *Back to the Future* and had traveled in his car time machine back in time. In Cuba, I saw few ads; there were very few visual assaults that distracted me from the city's magical, sunlit surrender to time. It was unlike most places in the Western world that visually attacked me with constant advertising of products and services.

In 2006, very few Cubans could afford smartphones or laptops; that kept them shielded from every form of visual assault, subconscious programing, and connection to the global portal of shared knowledge. Not communicating with the global world through e-mails, texts, Facebook, Instagram, Twitter, and so on kept them isolated from the rest of the world.

Yet when I got back in London, I knew that such a disconnect from technology, not sharing through social media, would constantly provoke insecurity and create anxiety that came from not always being connected and not in constant demand.

The more we develop as a society, what quiet and peace we have are always under attack. There have been reported cases of development work being stopped due to environmental impact, people being kicked off planes for refusing to shut down electronic gadgetry on take-off, or drivers being fined for talking while driving. Is this necessary?

I'm not one to clamor for continuous Internet access on buses, the underground, or on airplanes. When I travel, I love to relax, read a book, or converse with fellow travelers. I like getting on a plane, switching off my electronic devices, and greeting whatever news I am to receive onboard and getting to know fellow passengers. If I'm on a long flight, I love catching up on movies.

Daily, I use my bike, the underground, and other trains. I notice how most people on trains speak on their mobile phones and when they're underground, they feel fidgety because they can't check their Facebook status or use their mobiles.

For years, many people complained to the London underground why it didn't provide free Wi-Fi while undergrounds elsewhere did. Today, in almost every underground station in London, you can connect through Virgin's Wi-Fi network to the global portal of knowledge and communicate with others. It's remarkable. Hundreds of meters below the surface of the earth, we can connect to and communicate with the world. Being always connected to the Internet and through it to a global consciousness that's constantly evolving and shaping our lives has become the new norm.

Every big coffee chain such as Starbucks, Café Nero, or Costa Cafe provide free Internet access; this is of great benefit to customers and a clever marketing tool. But sometimes, I'd gladly sacrifice an Internet connection for not having to listen to someone nearby screaming, shouting, and swearing into his or her phone.

You may remember times in your childhood when you stared aimlessly at the sky, listened to the birds, and watched the sunlight playing on trees. You wondered about life in distant cities that promised a better tomorrow or otherwise engaged in the hopelessly antediluvian activity of wool gathering. You may recall how deliciously freeing it felt to wander fields, woods, or downtown for a few hours and knowing no one knew where you were. Today, in a world in which you're conditioned to always be switched on and connected to the Web, it's become difficult to replicate that same freeing experience.

Many of us meditate daily and take long walks or bike rides or go to our favorite places to spend time in solitude. I recommend that you commit to having a technology-free day. I like going to Macedonia to spend time with my mother, do gardening, and visit my mum's birthplace, Leunovo, a village in the mountains of western Macedonia. I pick up a spot by Lake Mavrovo, sit on a blanket, and let my entire being relax. I observe, soak up, and enjoy the energy radiated by Mother Nature away from the business of my busy daily life.

If you want to be the love you'd like to see in the world, act now to daily harmonize your inner being so it doesn't radiate toxicity. You will thus radiate love, the highest expression of your being. By such inner harmonization, you will elevate your existence and inspire those around you to do the same.

CHAPTER 8

TECHNOLOGICAL ARMAGEDDON IS AN EVOLUTIONARY NECESSITY

Stephen Hawking said, "Humans who are limited by slow biological evolution couldn't compete and would be superseded." Back to the present and on to the future. While I love technology and what it can do to help us improve the quality of our lives, let's not be naïve; let's examine the potential threats to humanity advancements in technology can bring.

In the duality chapter, I mentioned how every positive had a negative. In this chapter, I will shine light on the potential technological Armageddon we may be facing in the next fifty to a hundred years and what we can do in the present to turn things around so we can harness the benefits technology can bring us and our children.

While I love technology, I think about the dangers that advancements in technology pose to our survival. We're conditioned to rely more and more on technology; it's being introduced into every sphere of our lives. Wherever we turn, technology is there to make sure we're doing, thinking, feeling, and being what the people who designed these technologies want us to. Ask yourself, is living in peace important to me? Are my children's lives important to me? What about the importance of human connection, love, and freedom, are they equally important to you?

Imagine what would happen if the technologies we are creating exceeded our intelligence. This could lead to a robotic species that takes off on its own. Just as humans love to procreate, they too could start to redesign and replicate themselves. We humans, limited by slow, biological evolution, couldn't compete with advanced robots that had the ability to store, process, and recollect the worlds global information system in matter of seconds or even milliseconds.

These advanced robots wouldn't need to sleep, eat, or breathe, and in time, we'd be superseded by artificial intelligence (AI). No one knows at this time if we'd be infinitely helped by robots or ignored, sidelined, or conceivably destroyed by them.

This is a real danger we face globally, one that could lead to our extinction. Clever robots and other AI capable of undertaking our tasks could destroy millions of jobs. Today, some robots clean, cook, nurse, and manufacture things, and recently, a lifelike robot that welcomes visitors is at work in a Tokyo department store.

I'm not alone in fearing for the future of the planet; so do my friends, clients, and even Elon Musk, chief executive of rocket-maker Space X. He also fears that AI is "our biggest existential threat (Cellan-Jones, 2014)" and how it may affect our evolution.

World-renowned professor Stephen Hawking also fears this technological Armageddon. In a BBC interview, he talked about the benefits and dangers of the Internet: "The development of full artificial intelligence could spell the end of the human race."[7]

Science-fiction writers predict this extinction, as do sci-fi movies such as *Star Trek*, in which *Borg* was a proper noun for a fictional alien race that had been turned into cybernetic organisms functioning as drones in a hive mind called the Collective. The Borg used a process called assimilation to force other species into the Collective by violent injection of microscopic machines called nanoprobes.[8] Their ultimate goal was to achieve perfection.

Aside from being the main threat in *First Contact*, the Borg also played major roles in *The Next Generation* and the *Voyager* TV series as an invasion

---

[7]   www.bbc.co.uk/news/technology-30290540.

[8]   en.wikipedia.org/wiki/Borg_%28Star_Trek%29.

threat to the United Federation of Planets and served as the way home to the Alpha Quadrant for the isolated Federation starship *Voyager*.

As we continue to perfect AI, there is a real threat that in the near future, it will supersede human intelligence. Future humanoids will look like cyborgs—part electronic, part human. This may be the only safe way for humans to travel through space and survive high levels of radiation.

What I have described so far is no longer science fiction; we are there already. So many advancements in technology such as epigenetics, tissue replacement, and body-parts replacement are presently in use. This hybrid of humanoids and technology is only the beginning of what's to come.

Due to technological advancements, we may become even more segregated, ill, and lonely. We may even end up becoming extinct and living only in the memory of a computer chip designed by humans. Imagine that!

The consequences of this technological Armageddon for our consciousness are catastrophic. We'll see brain-stimulation patterns performed successfully by robots, all public services replaced by machines, and a high rise in unemployment globally. This could lead to further segregation and war and drive humanity to the wretched cave of solitude and eventually extinction.

Your relationships, your contentment, your sense of you, and your children's sense of themselves will not exist in a world dominated by AI. Rapid technological advancements could genetically modify the seeds of loneliness into hydrogen bombs that at a push of a button could destroy us all or send us back to the ice age.

We are slowly approaching an era of singularity where for many years there has been a theoretical emergence of a super-intelligence far more intelligent than human intelligence.

Since the studies on the subject have begun, singularity was seen as an occurrence beyond which events cannot be predicted since the capabilities and motivations of a super-intelligence would be difficult for the unaided human mind to comprehend. As you have read so far, the existential risks from the rise of AI are globally catastrophic risks that threaten the future of humanity.

Technology has its place in our evolution. The great thing is that there are now drones and robots that can plant entire forests with trees, do ironing, and help the elderly with daily tasks. Soon, you will see driverless cars, planes, and drones that deliver mail and other products to your doorstep. This could be a tremendous benefit to society, but unless we create alternatives, robots could take over humans' jobs and create increased poverty, unrest, and more global conflicts. The thought of this might force us into the cave of wretched solitude, produce global, irreversible, toxic effects on humanity, and make us lose control of our lives.

In my research to see the positive and the negative impact of this on the global consciousness, I read Nick Bostrom's *Super Intelligence: Paths, Dangers, and Strategies*. In this book, he shared how singularity will create more segregation, isolation, and loneliness and could be catastrophic for our existence.

He calls Singularity a "magnum opus"; his book is an attempt to chart it, awaken us to it, and make us aware of its dangers. He charts the near-inevitable rise of super-intelligence, and as you read it, you will imagine what might come as a result. Perhaps it is time to reflect on the direction we're taking our planet. We may conclude that if we continue evolving technology faster than the human consciousness evolves, our future doesn't look bright.

Futuristic thinking can be embarrassingly overimaginative or embarrassingly underimaginative. It can leave us feeling desperate, doubtful, disconnected, and fearful and at the same time hopeful, curious, and excited. Some visions of the future Nick described have elements of both: *Back to the Future Part II*, set in the then-distant future of 2015, features far-fetched scenes of cars flying, the Cubs winning the World Series, and fax machines, payphones, and laser discs.

Many visions I saw when I was unconscious in the hospital have become true. Among those visions were the civil war in former Yugoslavia, seeing myself living homeless on the streets of London, and writing an instruction manual to help humanity heal—my book *A Path to Wisdom*. Nonetheless, no one can firmly say that predictions of the future and the technological Armageddon will happen. They're just possibilities of multiple realities that are created by the choices of the collective human consciousness.

No one knows what's possible if we manage to find a way to unleash 100 percent the power of our brain let alone what will actually happen. But we do have the means to predict, calculate, and measure the impact that the rise of technology would have on our health, jobs, and the quality of our lives.

We can also use our imagination, creativity, and innate abilities to look at the many possibilities and the likelihood of their happening. With knowing this, we can also predict the effects it will have on our future, our well-being, and the way we live.

To make a prediction, we need to start from at least a few stable assumptions, but when we can't rely on these, the only honest prediction is just a humble shrug.

The possibility of the development of super-intelligence, an artificial mind, perhaps a robotic or an enhanced brain greater than ours is real. Super-intelligence would have such profound repercussions that its arrival has been hailed as the singularity. Certain nerd circles wait for it with a messianic zeal normally reserved for cold fusion or a new *Star Trek* or *Star Wars* movie.

Bostrom predicted that the singularity would happen in three stages. In stage one, humans would create an artificial, superhuman intelligence. You can imagine the segregation, loneliness, and isolation this could cause globally. People would end up competing for jobs, resources, and connections with artificially created intelligence that superseded human intelligence in every way.

In stage two, AI would decide to improve on our design and create a new version of itself that was even smarter. Now, this would be big; this would be where the beginning of our extinction as species would start and so would the birth of new, superhuman species we see in movies such *Supernatural* and *X-Men*.

In stage three, who knows? But it probably wouldn't end well for us. The problem is that people are being controlled by injecting fear into the global consciousness, the basic element that makes it easy to control, conquer, and manipulate masses.

When people can trigger fear in you that comes from your survival instincts, they can control you. Due to our survival instincts, we aren't aware of the changes taking place now worldwide that could lead to our extinction in a hundred years maximum.

The kind of super-intelligence I'm talking about ranges from brain emulation (think of Johnny Depp in *Transcendence*) to synthetic artificial intelligence in the movie *Ex Machina* and AI (Scarlett Johansson in *Her*) and biological enhancements through eugenics (Jude Law in *Gattaca*). Creating such super-intelligence that could supersede ours is no longer something we see only in science-fiction movies. It's being created today, and it's perhaps an inevitable reality we can no longer escape and will soon be the norm.

AI could develop rapidly; if we're not careful in the way it is designed, it might kill us depending on its goals and how we factor into them.

The key to turn this technological Armageddon into a favorable solution for our evolution is in its design and application and in the manner we seed the system with the right values. This way, the outcome might not be catastrophic.

What's at stake is the survival of the human race. If we and our descendants want a safe world, we must weigh the ethical and practical implications of super-intelligence as carefully as we consider, say, the implications of the Ebola virus, HIV, or nuclear war.

What role are you playing in creating global segregation, loneliness, and the technological Armageddon? What action can you take to safeguard the planet and humanity? You have the chance to change the future for better or worse. One choice, one decision, is all it takes to plant the seeds of a super-intelligence that could take over and lead us to extinction or create technologies that support the evolution of our human consciousness.

Imagine super-intelligence converting the universe into a computing machine to run simulations of people who are tortured forever in a computer-simulated life. What one thing would you want to do now to make sure that didn't happen?

By the time we develop this super-intelligence, the number of souls on earth could exceed ten billion. The true number is probably much larger, one that in our current awareness of life's universal and intergalactic existence we can't comprehend.

Doomsday scenarios are frightening and amusing. We don't know how super-intelligence might emerge and how we might be punished for failing to intervene. There are many theological ideas about how this could happen, picayune disagreements about whether the euphoria will occur before or after the great misfortune or whether the Second Coming will occur before or after the Golden Age.

The key eschatological question for us to consider at this key moment in history is whether super-intelligence will emerge slowly enough for us to realize what's happening (the slow take-off scenario) so we can correct the course of the planet and human evolution. It could emerge so quickly that we never get the chance to even predict whether one intelligence will come to dominate. Just as humans do, they might decide to share power.

This is food for thought, a wake-up call from me to you and from your soul to you about a possible future in which our fundamental notions of reality and consciousness will be subject to a radical overhaul.

The idea that super-intelligence might be possible is by no means a safe assumption. To maintain perfect equilibrium, for every scenario that technological advancement proves lifesaving, we can find a corresponding negative one that proves fatal to our existence as a species.

A self-modifying intelligence that improves itself is by nature chaotic in the sense that it will be extremely sensitive to its initial conditions. This is the equivalent of trying to stop a storm a thousand years from now by preventing a butterfly from flapping its wings today.

What if our inability to embed in the design certain values that can prevent this technological Armageddon happening causes the AI to judge us unworthy of existence? What if AI learns to be conscious, jealous, and emotional as we can be? If these scenarios sound far-fetched, recall that *far-fetched* is not a discrediting term in this book.

The problems raised by the singularity, loneliness, and everything else discussed so far in our journey touch on deep human anxieties that our existence is fleeting, that our meager intelligence seems to point to an order we can't comprehend, that technological mastery often comes at great expense to human life, and that perhaps we're unfit guardians of the planet.

The concerns raised so far in our journey exemplify a fear specific to what it means to be a parent, a guardian of human evolution, and a conscious creator. We fear that the next generation might surpass us and might not uphold our values or treat us kindly. Let's imagine that super-intelligent AIs are humanity's future children; how could we survive their rebellious phase?

Though it's hidden from your day-to-day living, the universe is expanding rapidly, and you too are going through periods of expansion and contraction. You're constantly evolving into a different species, and evolutionary loneliness is your constant companion through building and destroying life. If you're not mindful of technological advancement, you may be even more alone in the sense of not actually interacting with, looking at, or being in the presence of other human beings.

Globally, people communicate more through social media than meeting one another in person. You can't spend time with others on walks or at a restaurant if you're busy picking up messages from elsewhere. Our quest for technological advancements and to evade loneliness, disconnection, and death has made us more alone than ever.

I hope this book has equipped you to better experience life when put through the duality lens. You can see with clarity the dangers of the singularity and be inspired to take action. As you draw lessons from all life's adversities, you will awaken to the problems your inner separation can have on your decisions and well-being and on the evolution of your soul.

This is a call from your higher being to you to elevate your existence, learn the lessons, and pray, meditate, act, and counter the possible effects of this universal threat and the effects of your present actions.

Make a difference, connect with billions of people, and share this message, book, and this call for love. Choose to pave the path for the evolution of your soul, elevate your existence, and be the light guardian who safeguards our species. What each one of us collectively feeds the consciousness will determine the way we will live.

Since childhood and especially after publishing *A Path to Wisdom*, I was called to inspire people around the world to awaken to their inner truth and equilibrate their powerful minds with the divine will of God.

To contribute to global conscious shifts is to simply polish your mirror and reflect the inner light, love, and the divine will to the collective consciousness. The global segregation experienced is just a reflection of the disharmony created in you. This discord gives rise to the deep loneliness that can make you ill and combative and through advancements in technology make you irrelevant and extinct.

By shifting your inner world, balancing your emotions, and harnessing the power of your higher mind, you can contribute to stopping this virus of the modern age. You can ensure that the technological Armageddon is transformed into an evolutionary necessity for humanity. You have the power of many hydrogen bombs; by making positive shifts in yourself, you can harness this power to make a global difference. You can be the light that illuminates the path for lost souls to find their way back to living in gratitude, love, and certainty. You can make this global shift a reality in which we harness technology to help the evolution of humanity as it starts to explore the vast space outside our galaxy.

Living your life through balanced conscious choices increases your vibrational state. When you vibrate at higher frequencies, you overcome life adversities at a much faster rate. At this higher vibration the fears you may have, loneliness, and the disempowering beliefs that keep you from honoring your infinite abilities to be a creator of life become the fuel you need to help you evolve, create technologies that are cosmo-ethical, and move you toward the ocean of infinite wisdom.

Take the time now to clear the distractions that come from ever-increasing demands on your time, money, and attention. Address the real causes of your apparent loneliness, the virus of the modern age that keep you paralyzed, isolated, and disconnected from your true nature. Addictions such as sugar, drugs, alcohol, relationships, love, sex, gambling, and in recent years advancements in technology and social media can teach you to pause, reflect, and take back the reins of your life.

As more and more of you become aware and open your hearts to love, you will awaken the creator in you and honor God's will. You will feel connected to your infinite source of wisdom, stop thinking like a human, and start being the super-intelligence you know you are.

CHAPTER 9

AWAKEN YOUR TRUTH

To get to know the whole being that resides in you, the one with infinite abilities to grow, create, love, evolve, and transcend to higher states of awareness, you must listen to your inner alarm. Your body's intelligent feedback mechanism uses this alarm to awaken you to your truth and make you listen to the call for love that comes from the depth of your being. That love knows you're not aligned with or thinking like the eternal soul you are.

To elevate your existence, listen to your thoughts, values, and heart. This will start the harmonization process across your body, mind, heart, and soul that's required to align the power of your mind with the light of your heart.

A drop of water can create a ripple; so can each one of your thoughts, feelings, and emotions. The ripples you create are positive, negative, or neutral, and through the HEF, they spread into your environment. Depending in what state of consciousness you are in, the ripples you produce cause global toxic pollution or create waves of light that help neutralize the effects of the pollution caused by lopsided emotions.

When you live unconsciously, you don't acknowledge the effects of your way of being that lead to war and epidemics and perhaps even the technological Armageddon.

When you're not aware of the different conscious states, you live your life on snooze, don't listen from that place of love, and are unaware of your unethical behaviors that have global impact. Not expressing your true being makes you contribute to the extinction of the human race as we know it.

I worked in technology sector for over fifteen years and had to be a step ahead. I had to learn the latest technological advancements and how they can support the companies I worked for. I had to be up to date with the latest viruses to make sure a company's network was protected from those viruses. When I'd learn about a new virus, I'd study it and look at the network firewall, the gateway to the internal network, and make sure it was updated and protected against this threat. I studied the symptoms a specific virus would have on the network and individual computers. I learned to recognize infected devices so I could immediately take action.

I now often observe in people the same behaviors viruses had on networks. Loneliness affects people's well-being; it can paralyze them socially. Just like a computer virus, loneliness can enter a person and cause chaos. It multiplies through lopsided perceptions and unbalanced emotions, and through the HEF, it pollutes the global consciousness.

Just as a virus can paralyze a computer, loneliness can cause disconnect, fear, and doubt in people and lead them to the cave of wretched solitude. Just as a virus can shut down a whole network, loneliness in one person can infect others to whom that person is connected with that person's inner turmoil.

What would you do if you knew that every thought, emotion, and even the loneliness you may have are spreading the same way a computer virus does? Would you not want to stop the virus from infecting others? Would you not like to shift your inner state, equilibrate your mind, and raise your vibration to one that emits the antidote that cleans this virus and keeps you connected and living in a meaningful way?

You install antivirus programs in your computer; why not do the same and install a new way of thinking, being, feeling, and acting that will help you overcome your loneliness, transcend your mind, and elevate your being?

Knowing that you are a conscious creator, choose to install all the wisdom you have learned in our journey together. Let it be your antivirus program that cleans your negative, self-destructive, and disempowering ways of thinking, feeling, acting, and behaving. Let the truth that radiates from your heart become the antivirus program that cleans this global pollution coming from your loneliness.

Your toxic way of being is a consequence of the many viruses you have collected during your life. You have created the apparent loneliness you experience and emit, so only you can change your personal circumstances and positively impact the world.

Blogs, videos, and social media are both the ideal habitat for this virus of the modern age to breed, spread, and make us disconnect from our spiritual essence and the antidote you need to immunize yourself against this virus of the modern age.

Is it wise to use a computer that runs on an outdated operating system that has no antivirus software? You know its not! Would you rather use a state-of-the-art computer? Yes you would! Similarly, you cannot use your old, disempowering beliefs, unbalanced perceptions, and negative ways of being in today's demanding world in which you're expected to be a multitasker, perform at your best, and always be connected to the information superhighway.

Upgrade your consciousness; your new way of thinking creates a robust and secure operating system that automatically protects you from internal attacks from your subconscious mind and inner critic. It also safeguards you from external attacks that come from being always connected to others who may not realize their operating systems are infected.

You can connect with people who run their lives like outdated computers or be around people who operate with the newest hardware and the latest antivirus software. The choice is yours. The decisions you make and actions you take will stop this malicious virus from infecting your body and being radiated to the collective consciousness.

To stop infecting other people with negative emotions that spread at the speed of light and destroy the connections essential to the existence and evolution of our planet, you must harmonize your inner being, elevate your thoughts, upgrade your mind, and master your emotions.

Negative emotions allow spiritual, mental, physical, emotional, business, financial, relationship, and love issues into your life. Your inner truth knows this; as you learn to honor it, you will harmonize your body, mind, heart, and soul.

Research confirms the global impact loneliness has on the human consciousness and suggests it's more common in the developed countries such as the UK, those in the EU, and the United States. As mentioned earlier, Mother Teresa observed how lonely people in the United States were.

When polled in a 1984 questionnaire, participants most frequently reported having three close confidants. Interestingly, when the question was asked again in 2004, the greatest response was zero friends. Imagine what figures we'd have if that research were conducted today.

This unfortunate trend continues due to advancements in technology and AI. Experts believe that it's not the quantity of social interaction that combats loneliness but the quality of human connection. Having thousands of friends on Facebook won't cut it, but having just three or four close friends is enough to ward off loneliness and reduce the negative consequences associated with an unequilibrated state of mind.

Recently, a study, carried out by the BBC[9] and Comres suggests that 28 percent of British adults feel lonely at some time in their lives, 10 percent of those older than 65 expect to spend Christmas mostly on their own, and 33 percent say they feel left behind by new ways of communicating; 85 percent prefer speaking to friends and family face to face.

Loneliness can come and go or be a chronic condition. Most people who feel lonely don't acknowledge it or know they have it. It's a taboo subject many people are afraid to talk about for fear of being judged, ridiculed, or even rejected.

During a coaching consultation, my client Farhan described loneliness as "a gut-wrenching feeling, a void that nothing can fill." As did Farhan, many of you may feel this void and be afraid to speak your truth. You may lack the clarity, the awareness, and the skills required to detect it.

Knowing how behaviors, actions, and feelings are the seeds of loneliness is an art of its own. Many of you may be planting those seeds and living

---

[9]   www.bbc.co.uk/news/uk-30432939.

your life on snooze and not even realizing it; this is the time to awaken to the truth. Doing so will awaken your spiritual alarm that prompts you to act. The more you balance your perceptions, the more you raise your vibration. The more you do this, the better, faster, and easier it becomes to detect loneliness seeds in others.

Adam is another student of mine that experienced profound loneliness that led him on a path to speak his truth and honor his being. It is the journey that took him from living his life on snooze, being disconnected, ego driven, and lonely to being connected, experiencing unconditional love, and in balance. He learned every pillar of the TJS Evolutionary Method: the ALARM and embedded it his daily practice; in every coaching session we had, he awoke more to his inner truth.

He had known about but had never listened to his alarm. The way he was living polluted his inner being and in turn everyone around him. He radiated every pain and discord he experienced.

I met Adam during a Key Person of Influence (KPI) boat party in 2013; I had just finished it and Adam had just started it. KPI is a nine-month business accelerator program that helps entrepreneurs and business owners become key people in their industries. This is done through a simple and effective five-step process: pitch, publish, product, profile, and partnership. It is what helped me acknowledge and honor my value and listen to my truth.

It was a beautiful, clear night as we cruised majestically down the river Thames, enjoying a three-course meal with champagne, and listening to live music. We were with many amazing entrepreneurs at different stages in their entrepreneurial journeys.

Adam was a very charming entrepreneur, the youngest among us, and very good looking. He saw himself as someone who was extremely driven, thirsty to succeed, and ready to claim his Key Person of Influence title. The backflips he did as we were leaving the party got him a lot of attention.

He asked me what I did for living. I remember how I gazed peacefully into his eyes, observed the energy he was radiating, and responded with a loving smile, "I help people like you."

His eyes shrank. He became fearful and defensive. His positive, smiling attitude turned instantly into a negative one. As we continued to chat, he saw how one simple sentence had triggered his ego and his defenses to kick into full gear.

A part of Adam that was hurting wanted to angrily turn his back on me, but the curious part of him that wanted to learn, listen, and grow was stronger. It wasn't long before Adam let his defenses drop, put his ego to bed, and engaged with me in what he said was the most truthful, meaningful, and fulfilling conversation he'd ever had.

Our meeting created a chain of events that led him to change the course of his life. At the beginning of his coaching journey, he described himself as someone who had a business in health and fitness, did a bit of coaching and massage, and had strong views on how he was being the face of the raw vegan movement. Adam was very strong and acrobatic and frequently appeared on TV and in live performances.

To most of the world and in the circles of the vegan community, Adam appeared to have everything going for him. He had a huge fan base online, he received hundreds of thousands of views on his videos, and he had a relationship most would be envious of, his own flat at age twenty-two, and incredible health and fitness.

But as he started his coaching journey with me, he had to face the harsh reality that he felt completely alone, lived in an unfulfilling fantasy, was broke, and was constantly fighting to stay alive.

In many of our sessions, I sensed his strong desire to help the world from which he felt separated. He told me in detail his painful story; he wanted to save others from the pain he'd experienced since childhood.

Adam felt frustrated and lost; he had no clear vision in his personal, professional, or spiritual lives and no clarity on the direction his life was going. He experienced inner turmoil that caused pain, rejection, and loneliness he never truly acknowledged.

He'd spent much time, energy, and money on personal development, and he knew it was time to surrender the truths he'd started to unveil through learning and applying the TJS Evolutionary Method in the key areas of life.

He had faced the truth and chose to do the inner work he knew he had to do just before we met. In time, he started addressing the separations he saw all around him and how disharmony outside of him related to the inner work we have been doing for months. He knew that because he didn't acknowledge his internal separation, he was frustrated and disempowered.

One of the biggest internal separations Adam had to acknowledge was that he was being controlling by trying to bring the vegan diet and lifestyle to others. At the beginning of our coaching journey together Adam didn't know about the ego control games that were the cause of his feelings of loneliness, separation, and isolation from others. His fixed way of thinking kept him asleep and unaware of universal laws that apply to us all. By not respecting everyone's free will, he wasn't giving his heart the freedom it desired.

Untangling the limiting beliefs that supported some of his skewed perceptions, dissecting his inherited values, and equilibrating his mind helped him get rid of his desire to control others and take control of his inner world. He learned the importance of respecting spiritual laws and others' choices. He saw how he and everyone around him had been born with freedom of choice and free will. Adam's fixed views that the world would be a better place if everyone adopted his vegan lifestyle started becoming just memories.

As time passed, Adam faced his deep-rooted resistance to the differences in others' lifestyles. He came to understand how his nonacceptance of other people's freedom of choice was the cause of his pain and conflict with self and others. He realized that his thousands of followers were experiencing separation as well and were searching for answers to their inner conflict.

This separation, pain, and fear of being found out to be the lonely man he was is what I saw radiating from his inner being when we had first met. Having gone through a similar journey that led me to isolation and separation, I saw with clarity how Adam was facing what I had faced ten years previously.

Over the years, I've helped many clients awaken to their truth, overcome loneliness, and cope better with life adversities. I knew when Adam and I first met that beyond the separation Adam was experiencing, in his heart, he was a kind, loving, and accepting being ready to get out his self-made prison. I saw how deep down his drive to be of service came from a kindhearted place of wanting to make a difference from a place of love. Adam liked helping mistreated animals and was against people who killed them unnecessarily. He wanted to help people who were developing health problems due to their lifestyles and raise people's awareness of the impact a nonvegan lifestyle had on the environment as well as on people.

We explored the cause of his loneliness, segregation, and anger. He believed a plant-based diet was optimal for all humanity and didn't accept that not everyone wanted it. Over the years, these conflicting feelings and the nonacceptance of others' free will turned into sadness, feeling alone, and resentment of others and himself. Turning his focus inwardly for every life adversity he sought clarity about helped him eventually see how his fixed approach was controlling, disrespected people's freedom of choice, and further separated him from the people he was trying to help.

The more he started to listen to the voice that came from the depth of his being, the more he awaken his truth and the more he started to understand his personal contribution to the global consciousness of separation.

Adam acknowledged and shifted his many disempowering beliefs that had become the cause of the pain he saw in the world. He saw that the parts of him that weren't acknowledged or loved by others created his inner turmoil.

The more he awakened his truth, the more he started to transcend the volatile emotions that kept him imprisoned in the cave of solitude. Through our sessions, he experienced breakthroughs; he learned to handle his daily challenges. The inner pains that came to the surface upon our first meeting were later seen as lessons. He acknowledged them as the seeds planted during childhood that resulted in his feelings of rejection and nonacceptance that resulted in his anger.

Adam had always been connected to nature and loved the simple things in life. He wanted to love and didn't want to hurt or cause anybody pain. He always felt different; he never felt he could fit in with people who didn't think the same way.

His unpleasant childhood made him feel isolated, confused; he felt there was something fundamentally wrong with him. He tried for many years to change who he was to fit in with the rest of the world, but he always had to retreat from the pain he felt each time he tried and failed.

Every bad experience reconfirmed his lopsided emotions and led him to feel more lonely and isolated and to lose faith.

The trust we established during his initial consultation helped him create the safe space he needed to explore deeper the source of his wretched solitude, financial problems, and relationship challenges. This trust laid the foundation for him to do the work required to heal the wounded, critical, and fearful inner child and learn to play freely. Through this work, Adam saw clearly the source of his pain, loneliness, and anger, and that made him want to change.

At age eight, Adam had been taken away from the nature he loved and the environment he was accustomed to; he was put into a school he didn't enjoy, belong to, or wanted to be in. Being so young, he didn't understand that way of life. Adam was not at ease at school; he didn't feel loved, nurtured, or accepted, and he started to hide his truth and withdraw emotionally and physically from others, including his family. He embarked on a path that led to further isolation, loneliness, and adversities that forced him to hide in the cave of solitude.

He found refuge in street gangs and addictions such as smoking, alcohol, and shoplifting. He lived in fear of violence from other separated individuals who belonged to other gangs. He experienced many nights of complete aloneness living on the streets and always being responsible and strong and taking care of others. Of course, his harsh reality led Adam to mature very fast. He experienced many painful life lessons and developed empathy and an understanding for others' painful experiences.

The more time we spent getting him to open a dialogue with his inner child, the more he started to listen to his inner alarms and the more he connected the dots that drove him to be harsh, defensive, and extreme in the way he saw life and others.

Adam started to listen and heal his wounded inner child, he developed new habits, and he daily worked to bring into harmony his inner discord. He went from feeling alone, angry, and judgmental to being connected, calm, and accepting. He saw that by changing his inner state, he started to radiate the abundance he felt within that paved the way for him to uncover his soul's highest potential from a place of balance.

Noticing how balanced perceptions brought him back to feeling connected and loved and the inner knowing of his soul's mission of being of service to others, for the first time in his life, he was clear on what he was good at and wanted to be.

He wanted to help people achieve a state of inner balance from which they could grow further. Helping him awaken to his inner truth was all it took to turn his extraordinary personal journey to achieving a state of balance into a clear business vision he connected with. Exploring the depth of his being using the TJS Evolutionary Method: the ALARM led Adam to becoming the energy rebalancing coach.

He and I focused on unlocking the mountain of value he was sitting on, improve his amazing gifts, and develop his unique energy healing massage sessions to restore blocked energy into a state of balance. Through this trustworthy, transparent, and transformative journey as well as starting to coauthor a book in Mexico, Adam unlocked the final secrets and the inspiration to create and refine his energy rebalancing methodology and to write an amazing book.

After moving through and transcending the many layers of the ego, unbalanced perceptions, and the segregation he felt, Adam created the business he now loves, is authentic, and represents his true being. He focuses on daily actions, thoughts, and behaviors that keep him aligned to the light being and the love he knows he is.

The breakthrough Adam experienced through this journey together affected every sphere of his life. New people, opportunities, and experiences started showing up in his life. He felt worthy, nurtured, and uplifted. He noticed how daily practicing all he had learned on this journey helped him daily maintain his energy in balance. The more he was in balance, the more everyone around him felt at peace when they came in contact with him.

Adam learned to unlock the power of being present, truthful, and centered that he felt radiating from me when we first met. You too can be this positive influence that radiates from your being when you chose to operate at higher rate of vibration and from a place of balanced perceptions—love.

The power we can unleash through our choices and decisions can help us connect to our eternal beings easily. Through the power of unconditional love, freedom, and connection, we can positively affect the world around us.

Adam still enjoys a plant-based diet, but he now lives his life without the need to project outwardly, categorize himself or others, or intrude on other people's choices. He's genuinely happy and content with freedom of choice and free will and others' personal journeys. He approaches everyone with an openness that makes him a pleasure to be around and explore with. Adam awakened his truth, walked the path, and listened to his wake-up call. This helped him move away from the cave of wretched solitude and toward the oasis of elevated living.

He now knows that his work is authentic; he works daily to keep his energy clean, and he reflects on every experience to make sure he doesn't revert to his old self. His new routines, beliefs, and habits help him balance his perceptions so the negative emotions, inner self-critic, and loneliness that once ruled his life remain tamed.

Just like Adam, choose daily to make choices and decisions that support you in your personal and spiritual growth. Get yourself a good coach or a mentor that can be a great mirror for you to reflect, learn, and grow. There are many people out there who do some amazing job, let your heart attract the right person for you, and if I can be of service please do not hesitate to get in touch. In doing so, you too can change and heal your life. Every life adversity you wish to overcome starts with that one choice, one decision, or one action to change the direction your life is going.

I trust that the birth-given wisdom and the intelligence in you will awaken your inner truth, help you soak in everything I have shared, and immunize you against your apparent loneliness. Embrace now the new path you have been learning so far and decide in all you do to transcend your mind, elevate your being, and open your heart. Honor your truth, your voice, and your soul's true purpose.

Friendships, partnerships, and relationships are like the food we eat every day to nurture our bodies; we need them to survive, thrive, and grow. What's more important for us to acknowledge at this moment is our thirst for wanting more, being more, and giving more. It's a thirst that was there with us from birth and will be with us throughout our lives and constantly needs to be quenched.

Psychologists find that human beings have a fundamental need for inclusion in group life and for close relationships. This need drives us to connect, to belong, and to love. We are social animals; if we're not careful, we can easily spread the viruses (germs) that one-sided emotions can be.

Adam's personal journey is a good example of how one person who deep inside feels isolated, separated, and angry is like a virus that uncontrollably spreads into the global consciousness and causes toxic effects. Imagine how much toxicity billions of people who feel lonely, experience inner discord, and are unbalanced can create.

Our unbalanced perceptions fuel our emotions and keep us from awakening to this truth that creates the environment in which illness thrives. Harmonizing our bodies, minds, and souls helps us become the solution to the global segregation problem. It addresses illness at seed level, expands our cosmic vision, and lets us be of service by preventing the possible extinction of the human race.

CHAPTER 10

YOUR HEALTH IS YOUR GREATEST WEALTH

I hear stories daily about successful people who work very hard to accumulate wealth and in later years spent that wealth to heal the illnesses they've developed in the process of attaining that wealth.

The many successful people fortune has put on my path spent a lot of time working extremely hard to get what they wanted. In their quest to be more, have more, and achieve more, the majority end up feeling isolated from people who don't have similar values, drives, and desires. Loneliness takes over due to the constant pressures to fulfill the void within. Their way of being and living increases the risk of their developing severe illnesses and leads to all sorts of physical health issues, emotional problems, and in the worst case, premature death.

Many who seek my help do so after they've become ill or can't bear the emotional pain that comes from the depths of their being. Studies highlight the various health effects loneliness has on elderly people, but these effects aren't exclusive to the elderly; we all can experience them.

Those who are lonely tend to avoid contact with others and choose not to see friends or family regularly. They are almost 50 percent more likely to develop illnesses and die before their time than those who have people around them they love to spend quality time with.

In today's fast-paced and economically unstable world, many people end up living alone. Social as well as economic problems have forced even large companies to encourage their employees to work from home. Many people migrate to other countries to support their loved ones, make ends meet, and give themselves and their children a better future.

More and more people in metropolises around the world live alone due to their daily pressures, demands, and difficult personal circumstances. Some of you who are single may want to reconsider why you're manifesting that reality. Is it because you're avoiding pain and seeking pleasure, or is it because you don't want to open your heart for fear of being hurt again?

Research shows how living alone affects your health and increases the risk of suicide for young and old alike. Lonely individuals report higher levels of stress even when they're exposed to the same stressors as people who aren't lonely and even when they're relaxing. The social interaction lonely people lack means they don't have the buffers from stress those with relationships benefit from.

Loneliness raises blood pressure and levels of stress hormones; that undermines the regulation of the circulatory system so the heart works harder and the blood vessels are subject to damage by blood-flow turbulence.

Feeling alone also destroys the quality and efficiency of sleep so it's physically and psychologically less restorative. Lonely people wake up more at night and spend less time sleeping than do those who aren't lonely.

In *Loneliness: Human Nature and the Need for Social Connection*, authors John Cacioppo and William Patrick concluded that loneliness sets in motion a variety of "slowly unfolding pathophysiological processes. (Cacioppo, 2008)" The result is that the lonely experience higher levels of cumulative wear and tear. They found that loneliness hardens the arteries, which leads to high blood pressure, inflames the body, and causes problems with learning and memory. Even fruit flies that are isolated have worse health and die sooner than those that interact with others. This important research shows that the need for social engagement may be hardwired into our DNA and is essential to our survival.

Another study by Cacioppo and Steve Cole of UCLA concluded as I have that the immune system changes over time in people who were socially isolated; the researchers observed a change in the kinds of genes lonely people's immune systems were expressing.

Genes overexpressed in the loneliest individuals included many genes involved in immune-system activation and inflammation. In addition, several key gene sets were underexpressed, including those involved in antiviral responses and antibody production. The result is that a lonely person's body has let its defenses down to viral and other invaders.

They saw a consistent pattern of human immune cells being programmed with a defensive strategy that was activated in lonely people. I observe this in every client whose ability to vibrate love I helped raise. The more my clients increased their self-love, the less they were prone to flu and other illnesses.

This is because the immune system has to decide between fighting viral threats and protecting against bacterial invasions because it has a fixed capacity to engage in such battles. The immune systems of lonely people who see the world as a threatening place focus on bacterial rather than viral threats. Without antiviral protection and antibodies to fight illness, a person has less ability to fight cancers and other illnesses. Those who are socially isolated suffer from higher rates of mortality and higher rates of cancer, infection, and heart disease.

We have created a trillion-pound pharmaceutical industry to cope with the side effects of people simply living in fear, isolated from one another, and feeling lonely. These are problems we can heal instantly through creating the connections, the human touch, and the trust required to allow the flow of the life force of love.

In my personal journey and in my work with top world experts, I learned how loneliness raises levels of the stress hormone cortisol and blood pressure; one study showed that social isolation can push blood pressure into the danger zone for heart attacks and strokes. It undermines regulation of the circulatory system so the heart has to work harder and the blood vessels have to fight blood-flow turbulence. The cycle created by loneliness can be an out-of-control, downward spiral.

Studies by Cacioppo also found that lonely people tend to rate their social interactions more negatively and form worse impressions of people they meet. During the times I worked as a senior information technology director and now as a speaker, coach, mentor, healer, and spiritual teacher of inner wisdom, I've witnessed the enormous impact loneliness has on individuals, families, societies, and all countries.

If we don't reevaluate the way we are being, don't take responsibility for the consequences our internal states of being generate globally, and don't take action, we'll face global catastrophic effects that could put us in the cave of wretched solitude forever. We will see more obese people, physically ill people, and emotionally aroused people ready to take to the streets. If we don't face this global issue, we may see our health care system collapse due to a lack of the resources required to deal with an ever-increasing number of patients.

The toxic effects of the segregation caused by loneliness will spread and affect our businesses, families, personal relationships, finances, health, and our emotional well-being. We must not live our lives on snooze and further disconnect from the energy that keeps us healthy, alive, and connected to the power of our being and unconditional love.

The problems and the solutions I present in this book can destroy us all or create great health, wealth, and social harmony. We can choose what power we harness in ourselves, which animals we wish to feed, and what decisions we will make.

If not contained, your loneliness will spread to every sphere of your life and create further segregation that will make you an unfit custodian of your environment, everyone around you, and everything that is. You can plant the seeds that create the next generation of super-intelligent humans that will supersede us or plant the seeds that will help humanity harness technology to help human consciousness evolve.

Creating human bonds and connections and making healthy choices will help us all not feel lonely. It will reduce the number of people getting ill. If we don't, we'll create super-intelligent AI that might not uphold our values or treat us kindly; imagine the impact that would have on us.

Loneliness creates many dangers if we cultivate it; we must realize that loneliness is a deterrent to mental, emotional, and physical health. Loneliness is as much a global health risk as it is a personal one. It causes addictions, unhealthy behaviors, and premature death.

To be sentenced to isolation is the worst punishment we can undergo in prison. We are social animals by birth wired to connect; when these connections are threatened or unavailable, our nervous systems go haywire and many negative reactions follow. The effects of loneliness are lethal to you and everyone around. It can ravage your body and brain.

Andrew Steptoe, from University College London, in collaboration with UCL colleagues Aparna Shankar, Panayotes Demakakos, and Jane Wardle, studied the effects of isolation and loneliness on the survival rates of 6,500 adults fifty-two and older. Their findings showed that isolation and loneliness were associated with shorter survival time but that after adjusting for demographic, socioeconomic, and health factors, only isolation continued to significantly predict survival.

The results suggested that intervention to reduce isolation and increase levels of social contact and integration are likely to be particularly beneficial for older adults. Loneliness is important, but it may be more closely associated with other health and demographic risk factors.

This virus called loneliness isn't new; it's been with us for thousands of years and has aided our evolution. Now more than ever, we're starting to understand the true impact loneliness has on our health and our survival as a species.

In the late '50s, Dr. Frieda Fromm-Reichmann, a German psychiatrist and contemporary of Sigmund Freud who immigrated to America during World War II, wrote an essay on loneliness, a subject that had been mostly overlooked by other psychoanalysts up to then. Even Freud had touched on this subject only in passing. She wrote about inner forces that made her struggle with loneliness. This notion might have been with her because of a young, catatonic patient who began to communicate only after Fromm-Reichmann asked her how lonely she was. Frieda wrote,

She raised her hand with her thumb lifted, the other four fingers bent toward her palm. The thumb stood alone, isolated from the four hidden fingers. Fromm-Reichmann responded gently, "That lonely?" And at that, the woman's facial expression loosened up as though in great relief and gratitude, and her fingers opened. (Shulevitz, n.d.)

Fromm-Reichmann concluded that loneliness was at the heart of nearly all mental illnesses. Just as Mother Teresa did, she wrote that a lonely person was just about the most terrifying spectacle in the world. That statement resonated with my entire being. Just as her patient had, for many years, despite my business, success, and adventures, deep down I felt lonely in my heart and mind, and in the way I saw the world.

Many of therapists, doctors, and coaches I coach withdraw from emotionally unreachable patients because of the risk of being contaminated by them. They evade loneliness to escape feeling guilty about not admitting to themselves they experience loneliness.

Through various research, I learned that Frieda's 1959 essay "On Loneliness" became a foundational document in the fast-growing area of scientific research we call loneliness studies.

For centuries, we knew infectious diseases killed, but until now, we didn't know that germs spread them. Most of us intuitively know that being lonely hastens death, but until recent years, we haven't been able to explain how. A partial list of physical diseases thought to be caused or exacerbated by loneliness include Alzheimer's, obesity, diabetes, high blood pressure, heart disease, neurodegenerative diseases, and even cancer; tumors can metastasize faster in lonely people.[10] Long-lasting loneliness can make you sick and even kill you. Applying all you have learned is the key to helping you break through your loneliness.

The way you feel impacts the way you think, behave, act, and are in your day-to-day live. Feelings can wreak havoc on your body, mind, and heart and those of others. In some cases, emotional isolation ranks as high a risk factor for mortality as do addictions such as alcohol, drugs, and smoking.

While increase use of technology, social networks, and daily demands may be seen as the reason for the failure of addressing loneliness at the root, the solution to this global epidemic is in each one of us. If we take back the reins of our lives, we can collectively reduce the impact loneliness has on us. It's time to see loneliness as a public concern that has been with us in the past, is in the present, and will continue to be with us in the future. It's a global social problem that's the product of an excessively conformist culture and of a breakdown in social norms. It costs taxpayers, businesses, and governments the world over billions of pounds every year.

---

[10]   www.newrepublic.com/article/113176/science-loneliness-how-isolation-can-kill-you.

It's time for governments across the world to act now to avoid the catastrophic costs of the loneliness epidemic, which is as dangerous as any flu pandemic.

About 30 percent of Americans don't feel close to people; this number could be much higher if everyone were surveyed and honestly answered a questionnaire that could correctly identify people's true source of illness, emotional pain, and loneliness.

Loneliness fluctuates with age and personal and socioeconomic circumstances. It may affect the elderly to a greater degree, but it pervades the lives of people of all ages. To better understand loneliness and social isolation among older adults, AARP commissioned a national survey in 2010 of those over age forty-five. The study profiled older adults who were lonely and examined the relationships between loneliness and health, health behaviors, involvement in social networks and the use of technology for social communications and networking.

Key findings revealed that 35 percent of the respondents were categorized as lonely. Older adults reported lower rates of loneliness than those who were younger; 43 percent of those who were forty-five to forty-nine were lonely compared to 25 percent of those who were seventy and older. Married respondents were less likely to be lonely (29 percent) compared to never-married respondents (51 percent), and those with higher incomes were less likely to be lonely than those with lower incomes. Slightly more than one out of three adults forty-five and older reported being chronically lonely. A decade earlier, only one out of five said that. With baby boomers reaching retirement age at a rate of 10,000 a day, the number of lonely people around the globe will surely spike and could be in the billions.

Many UK polls support the call to action this book is. The finding of many experts also are aligned with this wake-up call of the global segregation that lets loneliness spread through the social network and become a worldwide epidemic.

A poll commissioned by BBC London showed that more than a quarter of Londoners said they feel lonely often or all the time. The same proportion of people who participated said there was little or no sense of community where they lived, and a third said they felt they didn't know their neighbors.

Another UK poll found that family doctors were ill equipped for the increasing epidemic of loneliness. Research has found significant numbers of lonely people attending GP surgeries, with doctors saying they are ill equipped to help them. A poll of UK GPs carried out for the Campaign to End Loneliness found that three-quarters of family doctors reported that between one and five patients a day attended their surgeries primarily because they were lonely. Worryingly, almost half the doctors questioned said they weren't confident they had the tools to help lonely patients; only 13 percent of doctors were confident they could be of help in this matter.

Some doctors reported even greater levels of loneliness among their patients; 11 percent of family doctors reported seeing up to ten patients a day they thought were lonely, and 4 percent of doctors said they saw more than ten lonely patients on an average day. And the sicker lonely people become, the more care they'll need.

What's most momentous about writing about loneliness is that it offers concrete proof obtained through the best empirical means that the poets and bluesmen and movie directors who for centuries have deplored the effects of loneliness on body and soul were right all along. W. H. Auden said, "We must love one another or die."

Loneliness has a wide range of negative effects on physical, emotional, and mental health as well as on spiritual growth, finances, relationships, and self-worth. The risks associated with loneliness are numerous.

- disconnection, withdrawal, and segregation from others
- increased stress levels, depression, and suicide
- low immunity, cardiovascular disease, and strokes
- altered brain function, decreased memory, and progression of Alzheimer's
- antisocial behavior, alcoholism, and drug abuse
- poor decision-making abilities, performance, and leadership
- living alone, small social networks, and low-quality social relationships
- marriage problems, increased divorce rates, and lack of intimacy

These are just a few of the areas in your life in which loneliness takes its toll. If we don't collectively act and target the people on the periphery, help repair their social networks, and help them create protective barriers against loneliness, our future as a species will be threatened. Wars, social unrest, and social inequality will erupt, as will the rise in AI and the need for super-humans.

Those who feel connected, have equilibrated minds, and are spiritually aware experience stable marriages, higher income, and higher educational status. People who elevate their beings work on themselves and like you are thirsty to quench their souls' thirst for wisdom, knowledge, and spiritual growth. The more you elevate your existence, the calmer, healthier, and richer you will become.

Remind your curious being that loneliness exists everywhere and is an evolutionary process. It's within you, society, at work, when you travel, when you socialize, when you do activities that involve others, in families, and in your closest circle—the personal relationships with self and those you are intimate with.

If you don't act now, it may be too late to do something about it once the singularity phase I discussed earlier is introduced into your day-to-day living. Your choices can cause the extinction of the human race as we know it and give birth to a new world in which AI decides to relegate us to the solitude of a computer chip.

Allow me to help you to get closer to your true seeds of inner discord and to recognize the many masks you may have created over the years that fuel loneliness and segregation and may cause illness.

In the next chapter, you will get to know the switch that activates your light. The next chapter isn't something you can "figure out" because it transcends thought. It's a case of letting go all the masks, definitions, and beliefs you have about yourself.

Give yourself this gift of light, clarity, and love. Equip yourself with the wisdom required to switch on your inner light and unleash your authentic self, equilibrate your mind, and own your personal power needed to create meaningful connections. It's time to activate your light that shines the path to your heart's desires.

Before you continue, make an intention to be a mirror for all others to reflect their own greatness. Right now, choose love to be your knight in shining armor and let this next chapter be your companion in this illuminating inner journey.

CHAPTER 11

KNOW THE SWITCH THAT ACTIVATES YOUR LIGHT

Now that you have equipped yourself with tremendous wisdom, done the exercises, and reflected, let's continue this journey with curious minds and open hearts. We will explore the subconscious part of yourself that activates your inner genius, switches on your inner light, and balances your mind.

Your reflections on the preceding chapters, the insights, and the lessons you have learned are great sources of knowledge to break through your loneliness, illness, and self-destructive patterns. The challenge for most of you is to remove the perceptions that prevent you from seeing how you already are in a switched-on state when adversity uninvitingly comes into your life.

When something negative happens to you that challenges your values, it's easy to unconsciously access this switched-off, disconnected state in which you defend your values that are being challenged. You default to old behaviors, thought patterns, and habits. You instantly feel lonely, not heard, and separated from your truth. You feel attacked and start to lose the confidence to connect with someone else, speak your truth, and share your angst.

You crave to be where you can feel alone, scream, write your thoughts, and reflect. You search for a place where you can learn to musically express your talents, listen to your inner voice, and find the key that unlocks your truth and activates your light. In this place of solitude, you feel inspired to unleash your creative abilities; you want to be the innovator, doctor, engineer, scientist, artist, writer, and designer you are so you can express your true self, shine the light, and unleash your infinite wisdom.

Just as you switch on a light to illuminate a room, you have an internal switch with which you can turn on your inner light and navigate the dark paths of your soul's journey.

When loneliness sneaks back into your life and you resist it, you're not allowing the flow of the life force in you. The love energy is there to keep you healthy, charged, and connected to the infinite source energy. If you don't know how to switch on your inner light to get this creative life force flowing out of your system and into existence, you're denying the creator within yourself. The disempowered parts of you that have been built over a lifetime build the walls of your inner prison that prevent you from seeing your inner light; you live in the dark.

Unless you know how to do this, all the wisdom you have collected through life, the light you are, and all the power that you as a god and a creator have are just stuck in you.

Knowing your infinite power, greatness, and abilities causes you to fear the disturbance in you that forces you to be constantly looking, searching, wanting, and needing something you think you don't have but desire to bring into your life. You continue to look for something that you deep down know you have but feel is securely locked in parts of yourself and hidden from your conscious awareness.

For this reason, you choose to invest in your personal and spiritual development. I believe that we all would benefit from a good coach, mentor, healer, teacher, or someone we trust who could help us navigate life's mazes. A good teacher can help us find our unique switches that turn on our inner light and teach us how to connect to this powerful, creative energy. I wrote this book to teach you how you can get to a place in yourself that is switched on, radiant, and truthful.

Honoring your inner truth, listening to your alarms, and opening your heart will help you find and activate this switch at will. The more you equilibrate your mind, the more your heart will open to the powerful force love is. You will thus become a teacher who helps others learn how to activate their inner lights and illuminate the darkest parts of their unconscious minds, where the seeds that create the fruits of their realities are.

This source of wretched solitude you're so desperately trying to overcome is an innate part of yourself. Just like many healthy bacteria in your body, it's there to serve you and keep you alive.

This is your call for the love that will awaken you to your authentic voice, the cry that comes from your place of solitude to remind you to plug back into the matrix of life, the divine source, the source of infinite energy, love, and wisdom.

Feelings of loneliness are your body's way of warning you about the consequences of your choices. They alert you to the switches you consciously or subconsciously switched off or on. The constant shifts between these two states keep you out of balance and lead you to places where you don't find the love and connection you desire.

Internal segregation brings to your awareness the situations in which you lack the physical stimulation you desire, the touch you crave, and the love you can unleash. Loneliness is there to bring to your awareness the presence of an inner switch with which you can turn off the addictions that make your body ill and stop it from functioning at its best. There are many other hidden switches that can turn on the light to show you blessings and miracles and help you return to a healthier state of being.

For electricity to flow freely, there must be a good wire and contacts; similarly, you need contact with your inner switch to activate the flow of your internal love force you need for trustworthy relationships to flourish. Trust, freedom of choice, and free will must be honored, respected, and cherished for a good connection to exist.

When you trust, the love energy in you will flow both ways; you will receive and give the energy you need to connect with others, share information, recharge, heal, and unconditionally love all that is within you and others.

At some time, a voice within, an inner knowing, a yearning will tell you when you aren't where you know you can be. Deep down, you know you're not fulfilling your true potential, you're not being the creator you know you are, and you're not living the life you were meant to live. This knowing will trigger the nagging feelings that contribute to the worthless part of you that is accustomed to loneliness, isolation, and fear.

Loneliness is a state of disconnection you experience and manifest into your outer reality. It's a state caused by a lack of awareness of the connection you have to your eternal spirit, your physical life, and your relationship with what's around you.

You can easily use the TJS Evolutionary Method: ALARM method to work through the protective layers you've built over the years and learn how easy it is to switch on the parts of yourself that know when there's something wrong with you or the things around you. As you switch on your inner light, you'll illuminate areas in your life that had been in darkness.

Understanding that you are the author of your feelings of lack of support and belonging is the first step in creating the change and the shifts you may be seeking right now. You can choose to turn on the switch of your inner light, see the disowned parts of yourself, and find ways to stop the wrong signals you may be generating that cause undesirable outcomes in your life.

Looking back, I clearly see how everything I endured in life gave me the awareness I offer you. The façades I built, the cave of solitude I entered, and the oasis I found were all part of this journey that helped me trust my journey and connect with my inner light.

If like me, the many people I have helped, and everyone on earth, you feel you aren't the person you deep down know you are, don't worry. It's all due to your past choices but an important part of your spiritual journey. The many façades you have built helped you hide your truth, pain, and authentic being in a desperate attempt to survive and feel safe, loved, and accepted. Being condemned, shamed, feared, and frowned upon by unbalanced, egotistical, and brainwashed people is a reflection of the unloved parts of yourself that require your attention and love.

People who project their thoughts, beliefs, and values from a place within themselves that's disconnected, unloved, and in pain are your teachers. Accept that you are a cocreator of that experience, acknowledge them for the lessons they are teaching you, and accept that you generate the signals that create your reality. Realizing this will free your trapped soul, open the doors to the miracles that come from living with gratitude, and let the light of your heart guide your path.

This inner disharmony causes illness, loneliness, and disconnection from others. Those with equilibrated minds, open heart, and curiosity don't use God as a façade, armor, or an excuse to fulfill their own agendas. They don't manipulate you to honor their intentions and values because they have aligned their inner power with God's will. The true masters are those who do not hold their truth in their actions but in their hearts.

Reaching higher levels of awareness helps you fulfill your inspired mission and shift from feeling responsible to knowing you have responsibility in adversity; you thereby honor the creator in you.

Examine your self-destructive behaviors; that will keep you from polluting the global consciousness. Observe situations through the eyes of love; that will keep you from adding fuel to war, conflict, and social economic differences that plague our planet. Your internal pain adds fuel to life's adversities and unconsciously separates you from the source and from others and pulls you into the cave of solitude.

When you're exposed to such toxicity, your inbuilt emotional guiding system knows how to save you. Listen to your inbuilt alarm warning you about your toxic environment and drawing you to the oasis of love. Acknowledging your infinite abilities to love will set you free to be the creator with infinite power you are.

As you look at the seeds of your loneliness, you will know that it is created by your inner disharmony that energetically, mentally, physically, emotionally, and spiritually has created your feelings of disconnect. Consciously or subconsciously, you have switched off the light and have given permission to your darkness to take over your life. In the absence of light, you go on a path on which every experience you have leads only to more separation and loneliness. Use your willpower to switch on your inner light; you'll find a way out of darkness and to the oasis of connected life.

Architects make sure that the buildings they design have the supporting structure they require. The know that if they don't, the buildings will collapse. If you don't have trustworthy, emotionally stable, and healthy foundations in yourself that support you, you will eventually collapse as well. You will lose the trust, confidence, strength, and clarity you need to recognize the magnificent being you are.

Of course you can be alone and feel comfortable with that. But when you realize you don't have inner resilience and strength, your aloneness turns into loneliness. You often see people enjoying being alone, say, in a park; of course we all need some alone time, but it becomes unhealthy if you use it as a way to hide your loneliness and not connect with others.

The one significant change in people's behavior I observe more and more wherever I travel is that talking to strangers is now considered by many to be weird, rude, and a violation of privacy. It's ironic that so many communicate and connect through social media and technology but don't strike up conversations with passers-by. It's no wonder why loneliness is at staggering levels in every sphere of our lives. In the '70s, during my childhood, we weren't distracted by fast-paced life, technology, and computer games. We'd talk to strangers, to neighbors, fellow travelers, classmates, and others we met daily. This is the time to listen to the voice within, to your heart, and allow yourself to bring human interactions back into your life—consider the power in a hug and the healing power of touch.

Practicing mindfulness daily will still your mind, open your heart, and encourage you to connect with even strangers. You can share a smile, receive a hug, and use your unconditional love to be the balm for someone's wound. In this one loving action you too can become someone's antidote and immunize them against loneliness-the virus of the modern age. You will thus be of service and honor the infinite love being that resides in your heart. The being that knows the God given healing power that lives in your heart.

Performing random acts of kindness will get you out of your comfort zone, increase the flow of your life force, and vibrate love and gratitude. Do something you've never done before, incorporate it in your daily gratitude ritual, and see how that inner light automatically switches on in the presence of gratitude. Through meditation, you can get to that place within where you become mindful, with ease switch on the light, and feel amazing being alone in the stillness of each breath you take.

When you reach this place within, you will discover the power in you that can bring you closer to the creator within and to life itself. You will unlock your innate healing abilities, develop your intuition, and expand the awareness of your true self.

Nature is a great reminder of your innate ability to destroy and create life. Reaching a place within where you consciously feed that part of you will help you be more connected, grounded, and centered; that's what this journey is all about.

With practice, daily meditation and listening to your inner alarm will activate your inner light switch and find a place within where you don't feel alone but rather connected and inspired; you will radiate the life force of love.

Most of you have been through breakups, arguments, expectations, fears, controls, and various challenges that have caused you to consciously or subconsciously withdraw from everything to heal and protect yourself and feel safe. But that makes you create the void, the darkness, and the isolation that come from loss of contact and touch.

Give yourself permission to use your infinite, God-given power to take control of your life and turn on your inner switch that activates your light, your love. You will develop new thought patterns, habits, and ways of being that help you learn, grow, and transcend loneliness, expand your consciousness, and elevate your being.

Becoming aware of, listening to, and acting on the messages from your inner alarm will help you find the different switches in yourself. You will learn what stops you from using your abilities to give, connect to, and receive from the world. You will awaken to your apparent disconnection from the divine energy, other people, and your eternal soul. Refocus your attention, listen to all the alerts your body gives you, and create new thought patterns; this will allow you to create new, empowering behaviors and habits that honor your freedom, trustworthy connections, and the infinite wisdom love is.

When you take 100 percent ownership of your life, you will realize how you are the energy vampire you complain about and how the way you are gives off the signal that invites into your life other vampires that deplete your energy and your life force.

Looking deeper within the self for the answers to your loneliness brings you to a place of true acknowledgment, a place where a lesson is born, and a state within where gratitude becomes your default attitude.

What you have learned in life teaches you how you lose your power and your ability to connect to your inner light. It teaches you that you can give your power away or hold onto it. You can decide to trust your authentic voice, the voice that knows about this separation and is there for you to learn from.

Your inner voids allow loneliness to creep into every sphere of life and make you feel something's missing. You end up feeling lonely even in a crowded pub, on the underground, at parties, and even in your relationships with loved ones and yourself. When you relate to this feeling, you're in fact giving it energy. Refocus your mind and bring yourself back into the present. Deep down, you know you can refocus your thoughts, so honor that knowing and see how your loneliness becomes connectedness. Negative self-talk plants the seeds that grow into gigantic trees of loneliness you don't want in your spiritual garden.

The moment you share, care, and dare to express your highest version of yourself with another is the moment you feel alive, acknowledged, appreciated, and valued. Next time a stranger asks you for directions and you help that person, notice how that makes you feel present, connected, and of service. Notice how your body feels good to have shared the wisdom you have and to bring clarity to someone else. Being grounded and being of service to others makes you feel alive, inspired, and in alignment with your authentic being every moment regardless of the people or situations around you.

Balancing your perceptions daily through always looking at the benefits and the drawbacks in every situation, person, and opportunity will ensure you'll remain centered, present, and certain. You won't feel stuck, alone, isolated, separated, or disconnected. Let yourself feel the loneliness for a short time, allow the awareness of this space to elevate your being, and switch on that connection within yourself that illuminates your heart.

Honor the power the duality of your nature is teaching you, harness the power of your perceptions, and see how easy it is to remove the seeds you plant daily with your choices and decisions. As you do so, you are equipped with the wisdom that enables you to instantly find the switch that turns on the love current, creates that contact, and makes the required connections for this love to flow. Each brain cell, organ, and organism in your body is immersed in the healing power of your love. The more this flow of love becomes unrestricted, the more your light shines brightly.

Choosing to walk the path of the old sages, the one I have been sharing with you and the one that your heart desires, will bring you closer to the miracles you desire, the love you admire, and the material wealth you aspire to. This shift within you turns everyone and everything around you that you may perceive as a threat into allies, teachers, and conscious cocreators of life.

As a child, you had an uninhibited mind, but as you grew up, you learned to forget about your free spirit, curiosity, and extrasensory abilities. You learn to be a rational being that lost touch with the child within and your childlike qualities. Observe children's behavior and ways of being, there is a lot for you to learn about activating, embracing, and harnessing the power of your forgotten abilities.

Children in general are able to connect easily to play with one another; they are also good at connecting with what may seem imaginary friends but can be angels and spirit guides. Adults tend to judge and criticize this behavior; if you speak of such encounters, you'll be treated the same way. But those who have developed their ESP are able to make contact with entities that live on another dimension unaware to most people. I've met many people who have chosen to develop their ESP and honor these childlike behaviors that lead to such profound, life-changing experiences and to live in a reality as real as the one you may be experiencing right now.

Knowledge is power, but applied knowledge is the wisdom required to honor your ability to give and receive love. Developing your psychic powers is a choice like any other choice you make. Meditation, equilibrating your mind, and developing your ability to connect to your pineal gland, which many spiritual teachers and healers consider your spiritual antenna, can help you activate and awaken your extrasensory powers.

Working through the perceived misalignments, clearing out the weeds discussed so far, and turning life adversities into lessons enable you to reach higher level of consciousness while still remaining grounded in the material world.

Accessing a reality children can will easily connect you to spirit guides, higher states of consciousness, and angelic realms that guide, nurture, and protect you through times when you disconnect from the source of love, the light within, and you feel lonely and with no one to turn to.

Unlike your fearful adult self, your inner child loves to be free, play, and have fun. Your inner child is curious to learn about life through this switched-on, curious state that we are all born with but have forgotten to use. Naturally, when you serve another person, when you help another person, when you connect and play with another person, your soul is free to express its talents, knowledge, and wisdom.

Becoming self-centered can lead to dangerous endeavors that are the source of the loneliness you're trying to escape. Spending most of your time thinking about yourself and ignoring your surroundings and the people around you who might need your support, love, and care will keep you chained in your self-made prison. However, being connected, present, and centered, you radiate pure love. In this state of flow, it's impossible to feel lonely.

Be cautious in the society in which you have significant levels of external expectations or an external sense of self-image not based on your personal values but on what you believe to be somebody else's ideals; you can easily be willed into entering the dark cave of solitude.

The lack of self-recognition you require from others to validate your self-worth gives birth to feelings of not being good enough and not up to certain idealized standards you may have learned at a young age. This feeling switches on the darkness that leads you to a poor self-image. You compare yourself worth with those you are infatuated with, you create a mask that prevents you from authentically connecting with others, and you lack self-worthiness and undervalue your true worth.

Comparing yourself to others creates the feeling of your worth in relationship to others. When you don't see yourself as an equal to others, you separate and disconnect from fear of your own greatness or flaws. You lack a sense of belonging and feel rejected, lonely, and abandoned. In this disempowered state, you live in the shadows of your magnificent light.

Being authentic and being yourself is something that is very commonly talked about today. As I addressed the difference between being an authentic being and the social masks that I learned to live with, I opened my heart to the infinite wisdom in me and in everything around me.

Equilibrating your mind helps you see life for what it is. You learn not to minimize or exaggerate yourself or others. You know in doing you lose your authenticity by creating a mask and become someone not entirely you.

Learning TJS Evolutionary Method and applying it in all that I have shared so far helps you in your journey to be authentic, living your truth, putting people in your heart with reflective awareness, and living congruent to what is most important to you. This is the key to unleashing the true leader in you, awakening your inner doctor, and living and elevated, fulfilled life.

You'll make the greatest difference to you and the world around you by being your true, authentic self, so use all you have learned so far to make the choices and decisions and shed the personae that prevent you from becoming your most inspired, fulfilled, empowered, and authentic self.

You are born alone, live most of your life in some form of isolation, and die alone. However, you find it difficult to accept loneliness as part of your evolution. The feelings of being rejected, abandoned, and alone are simply there as guides to help you unveil your authentic self you were born to be. Make the choice to acknowledge, accept, and love the experience of separation that happens at birth and is your constant life companion. From the moment of your separation from the source, your mother's womb, your perceptions become skewed and you learn to feel lonely, abandoned, and disconnected from the divine energy that love is.

As time passes, you forget who you really are, yet the divine wisdom within knows the infinite nature of your being and remembers the free spirit you know you are.

It is the divine within that bridges the gap between the feeling of being separated and your true self. The power of love brings you closer to your loved ones, to the oneness that life is, and to everything you came here to have, create, and be.

Loneliness is a complex issue whose source is at times difficult to recognize as it is well hidden from your conscious awareness. It expresses itself through many ways in all the eight key areas of life. Usually, it expresses itself in your life as an unpleasant emotional response such as feeling isolated, abandoned, judged, and rejected. It shows up in your relationships as lack of perceived connection, intimacy, and companionship.

Much of my research and my personal experiences and those of people I have helped have taught me that loneliness is not just something that affects individuals, but it also pervades people in marriages, relationships, families, friends, various groups, at work, and even in people who have successful careers and material wealth. It has been a long-explored theme in literature since classical days. If you do not choose to live from the place of gratitude, you end up seeing loneliness as social pain. If you do shift to higher levels of awareness, you see loneliness as a psychological mechanism that is meant to alert you to your isolation and motivate you to seek social connections that nurture your being.

Taking some time to answer some of the key fundamental questions below is what aids you in turning on the light switch I have mentioned that will shine light on the path your wondrous spirit is taking. Here are some "lightbulb" questions for you to answer.

- Why do you choose not to communicate with others when you wake up, leave home, are on your way to work on the tube or bus, at work, in your favorite coffee shop, on the streets, and so on?

- Why do you make your mobile phone, laptop, and other electronic gadgets your best friends to whom you turn when you're lonely and the places you hide when you crave intimacy, contact, and touch?

- With whom do you love to communicate your authentic self and why?

- Why is it important for you to switch on your inner light bulb and shine your light?

- What traits, qualities, and values can you adopt to activate your light switch and illuminate your path?

The insights you will gather from answering these questions will let you know what you can do daily to activate your light, remain in a switched-on state, and allow your love to flow so your body, mind, heart, and soul connections are harmonized. This harmonization brings healing to you and everyone around you.

Technology is changing and shaping the way you communicate, perceive things, and do things. It also shapes your innate behaviors in the way you connect, share, and are with others. Technology, if not used correctly, unconsciously programs your subconscious mind without your knowing the long-term impact on your well-being, material wealth, and the collective consciousness. With the exponential increase in technological innovations designed to help us connect, communicate, and engage better comes a decrease in human interaction, connection, and physical caring for one another.

Next time you go for a coffee, travel, or are out dinning, instead of being glued to your mobile desperate to connect with someone on the other side of the world, make a conscious effort to connect to the person next to you. Share this journey with the people you come across daily and let them know the importance of social interaction has on healing ourselves and our planet.

This is the irony of living a modern life; on one hand, you participate in creating so many innovative communication solutions, but on the other, you lose touch with your human abilities to connect, communicate, and share your presence, love, and touch with others.

Isolating yourself from the people you come across daily leads only to building many more façades to hide behind, creating more layers that eventually become thick walls, and encouraging new behaviors that later become difficult to spot and change.

The good news is many people worldwide are awakening to this lack of understanding how unconsciously they are helping create a reality that may lead us all to living a lives in which robots become our pets, friends, and partners and vice versa. It will be a reality in which AI in the near future takes over and may lead the human race to extinction.

Many of you like me may grew up in the '70s and '80s; back then, we didn't have mobile phones. Instead, we talked to one another. We would spend time to connect deeply and devote quality time to one another. We were free of the technological demands of today.

In contrast, today, we text and Facebook each other and hardly have the time to make human contact with others. I trust that you consider all you have read as a call for love, a call for you to awaken your being to the dangers that come from living in a disconnected, disempowered, and disillusioned state of being.

We are meant to improve the way we communicate, but the truth is there is less and less human connection at the end of the line. Call your bank, mobile provider, or any service provider and see how you are greeted with an automated answering message with choices of the next steps. If you are lucky, after spending a lot of time waiting for a human to answer your query, a person from another part of the world will pick up the call and ask, "How can I help you?"

However, if you are not that lucky, you end up feeling frustrated, angry, and disappointed. At some point, some of you hang up, learn the lesson, and take action to do something about it. You eventually change the service provider in the hope of finding a better connection and customer service.

This kind of automation while has many business benefits, it is essential not to be blind to the negative impact it generates. It creates a segregation that comes from the lack of human contact, understanding, and feeling. It also fuels further distrust and isolates you as the customer from the provider. In the race to increase their profits, many companies forget this very important fact: it's because of the people who spend their hard-earned cash that they are in business.

In my fifteen years of working in the corporate world, I saw how this lack of human contact, transparency, and automated telephone services fueled distrust, burned bridges, and created a reality in which employees and customers alike switch off their inner lights as they start to feel unworthy, uncared, and unloved.

As we continue to advance society through providing better technologies and more automated services, we must see the benefits and the drawbacks alike. If we don't see the two sides, we add fuel to the fire our children will need to extinguish.

You can easily avoid many problems but fail to because of the increased demands for your time. It is this constant demand for your time that makes many feel pressured, stressed, and ill due to the expectation to do more in less time. You start to lose parts of yourself that you once loved and the skills you once used that have become redundant and have been replaced, and eventually, you feel forgotten, abandoned, and rejected.

Remember your infinite innate abilities; you can inspire your inner being to reach out, make contact, and share. In being of service to others, you use the power of gratitude to turn on the switch that activates your inner light.

Acknowledging the power of your love makes your once-disempowered self become a distant memory, something that is unreachable, unrealistic, and unwanted anymore. Doing this collectively is what creates the change you so desperately want to see in your world. As we join in gratitude, we create the life force that cultivates the love seeds, harnesses the power of our minds, and creates the wisdom that is essential to our survival.

In today's fast-paced world in which the demand for your time has never been so great, if you're not careful, you can slowly create the conditions for the source of this wretched solitude to uninvitingly enter, change, and shape your life in most settled and yet painful ways.

You spend most of your time communicating through technology, yet you find it hard to switch off the need to be constantly connected to the same world that distracts you from honoring yourself.

You know if you treat electricity the same way and leave everything in your homes switched on, it will cost you the earth in electricity bills. Similarly, spending long amount of times feeling lonely, depressed, and disempowered drains your energy, and the cost to you is physical or emotional illness.

You were created with a self-generated system of charging; this system also has the alarm that warns you about abusing your body, mind, heart, and soul. Unlike electricity, the payment is not in money but in illness, the highest cost to your being.

Knowing this, choose now to adopt behaviors that stop you from carelessly doing things in your life that you know will cost you your health. Listen to your knowing, and acknowledge it by taking the action required to honor that knowing.

If everyone used electricity at all times, the planet's electricity grid would become overloaded, and all the world's power stations wouldn't be able to cope with this increased electricity demand. One by one, due to overload, they would start to shut down. Similarly, imagine the chaos that this kind of careless behavior within you that leaves you lifeless, feeling drained, and alone would create for your inner being, your health, and the workings of your body.

Your body's intelligence is constantly alerting you to change your way of being, to address the issues that take power from you, and to save your energy in every possible way. Not listening to this is what eventually leads you to be in darkness, on a downward spiral, and feeling alone in the coldness of the wretched cave of solitude.

Use your body's innate alarm to learn, awaken yourself, and to act when you are not being caring with yourself by overloading your body with more than it can handle. It is this warning that will awaken you to take back the reins of your life, conserve your energy, and appreciate your life.

Your truth is there to aid you to acknowledge to yourself a very important life changing fact—the healing power of love, gratitude, and human touch. You now live in the world in which daily you touch your phone, PC, and other devices more than you touch people who are the closest to you. It is up to you to maintain a healthy balance and use your human qualities to interact with others and be of service.

The effects of your inner separation are reflected in your physical and emotional health and everything and everybody around you, including your habits. Make the conscious choices required for you to cope better in the way you now live your daily, busy life.

The other day, I was asked to go to a primary school to coach the head teacher who was having issues with staff poor performance and stress and wanted me to deliver a talk and be a role model to a group of ten- to sixteen-year-olds.

I saw how much schools have changed since my days at school in the '70s, '80s, and '90s. Most children had mobile phones, iPads, and laptops. They spent a considerable amount of time on social media, playing computer games, and using various apps to connect, share, and learn. They also had their course work given to them in a digital format on their iPads.

It was pretty amazing when I compared that to my experiences in school or my parents' time in school. Although it may seem a long time ago, the truth is it is only forty years or so that children at school didn't have Internet, mobile phones, and iPads to do their work or get distracted by.

While we all know how important it is to embrace technology, we must not forget how important it is for children to learn to socialize, be with others, and converse without using technology.

What came out from the workshop was alarming and inspiring. On one hand, many children felt they had to conform to feel accepted; on the other hand, it was inspiring to see how they used technology to overcome rejection and social separation and find social groups in which they felt nurtured.

Some children did not know how to bond outside the social media with others; some felt a bit distant, and very few had the ability to confidently and openly talk about their concerns. Many have already started to lose their ability to relate to others, to connect easily with strangers, to touch, and to love and be present in the field that love is.

This wretched solitude people around the world are experiencing goes beyond what I saw in the school, what I see when I travel on the tube, and what many of my corporate clients whom I coach experience. It is so much more complex and so much more present in every layer of our society that we would like to think and have been led to believe.

Now you know how important it was for you to go on this journey to get you to the root of your loneliness. You equipped yourself with a tool that turns the lonely feeling that drains the life out of you and causes you many physical and emotional imbalances in your life force that propels you to reach out for your dreams.

Continue to speak your truth, walk an elevated path, and daily balance your emotions. See how this awareness of your eternal being is with you every moment of your life and is there to help you see loneliness as part of your wholeness.

Loving your lonely seeds that cause you adopt thoughts, beliefs, behaviors and actions that have the destructive power of an atomic bomb will turn them into an unlimited supply of energy for you to recharge daily and go on with your daily life.

With the speed of light, a single push of a button, in a split second, you can unleash your ability either to destroy life or create it.

If your loneliness comes without the craving for others' approval, without the need for others to fill the voids you are experiencing within, acknowledge to yourself that loneliness is not necessarily a bad thing. It is a teacher that can help you cope better with the amount of destructive forces that in the first instance come from the rejected, uncared, and unloved part of your being.

Accepting your loneliness has a positive effect on your life, well-being, and the collective consciousness. It helps you navigate back to stillness, inner peace, and bliss. Being at peace with being alone helps you learn to be at peace with other people. It is the solution to global segregation, war, and many socioeconomic problems.

Next time you experience loneliness, look deeper at the messages that are being communicated to you through your loneliness. In doing so, you will find the truth that you never expressed and trace back to that moment when you gave birth to your loneliness, the moment you created the thoughts, feelings, habits, and behaviors that created discord within you. That was when your unconditional love awakened you to take decisive action.

You have come toward the end of our journey together. Acknowledge the infinite wisdom in you that knows you are not a finite, tiny being who has only occasional glimpses of your spirit. Celebrate the truth that you are a spiritual being with infinite nature, abilities, and power who is having a temporary experience. Amplify your senses, listen to your authentic truth, and use your infinite power to turn the source of your personal loneliness into seeds of love for your eternal existence.

Hear clearly the voice within that is shouting at you; give it your attention, and let it help you connect the dots in your life where you may have experienced a perception of rejection, heartache, and apparent inner loneliness.

Acknowledge this voice, let the feeling of your loneliness pass through you, and as it does so, let your light disperse the shadows it lives behind. Surround any one-sided, negative emotions in a bubble that is full of violet light and see it become light, the energy of love.

It is only when these feelings are defused, your emotions are balanced, and your mind is equilibrated that you will experience a moment of divine love. You will experience an exquisite aloneness that will benefit you by building that inner resilience, internal strength, and flow that enables you to enjoy and benefit from the nurturing fruits that ripen in your times of solitude.

Be aware that if you're not yet at that stage where you are resilient enough, then aloneness can be toxic for you and will impact negatively the environment in which you are in that present moment.

If you don't have trustworthy connections with self, you lack that inner awareness required for you to see it on others. Build your strength, inner resilience, and trustworthy connections to keep yourself safe from the dangerous situations that you choose to put yourself into. You will instantly recognize those environments that aren't necessarily the best for you and keep yourself safe from being infected by other people's loneliness.

The key to neutralizing those unbalanced emotions is finding in each emotion the hidden order, how it is serving you, and what blessings it is bringing into your life. Learn the TJS Evolutionary Method to help you make a good inventory of the inner workings of your body, uncover the disowned parts of you, and face the lies that prevent you from living your truth. In the process, you will immerse with love on both sides of the coin (emotions), balance your perceptions, and find reasons why you can appreciate every situation you find yourself in.

Over time, the more you give yourself permission to evolve, love, and transcend the toxic effect that deceptive loneliness has on your life, the more you will come to the conclusion that in every environment you find yourself, you can instantly see both the drawbacks and the benefits. This will enable you to turn on your inner light and create the opportunity to connect, learn, and grow.

Experiencing the rejection from certain environments will give you the knowledge you will need to adapt to the new environment. You will learn the lessons you need to actively choose, create, and find new environments and people with whom you vibrate at a similar frequency.

The longer you stay dwelling in one-sided emotions, the more you will feed your disempowered self. Despite knowing that an environment might be unhealthy for you, you do not act on your knowing; instead, you try to fill the void by making contact with other people whose vibrations are similar to yours.

For some of you, your old ways of being can easily pull you back in a desperate attempt to avoid feeling alone, lonely or disconnected from the world and other people. It is a learned behavior, a habit of falling back to familiarity that turns off your inner light switch and the reason you remain in the darkness of your own creation. Make a note of what it is for you and create a new habit and new behaviors to support yourself in your journey to break through your loneliness.

Wherever you look, you are faced with situations, people, and environments in which you are being controlled and mentally "raped" through transmission of all the emotions, desires, and thoughts that come from billions of people with whom you are coliving. You take physical rape very seriously, but you ignore the mental rape you are subjected to daily by the influx of trillions of thoughts and information thrown at you that influence your emotions and most important your physical, mental, and emotional well-being.

Clearly, it's not the ideal life for you to be living, but you are. With evolution also come more distractions that are generated by a huge amount of products that demand your attention and time and put unreasonable demands on your energy.

It is for this reason that you should awaken your inner wisdom to support you, help you cope better with the pressures of modern life, help you live your soul's dreams, and breathe them into your physical reality. Make the choices that assist you in restoring your personal balance and health, and coping better with the noise that prevents you from embracing and accepting other people in a loving and nurturing way.

I have interviewed many people about their experiences of loneliness and have discovered that for the sake of survival and sanity, some felt it was better to expose it and let themselves be taken advantage of than to be completely alone and cut off. Some people are in relationships that deep down they know are toxic, but they never have the courage to walk away due to the persistent fear of being alone, judged, or ridiculed.

It's alarming to know that many people in the world simply accept the adversity that comes from living with someone who abuses them, takes advantage of them, and controls them due to their fear of being on their own and alone.

For some people, interestingly, this fear of being alone is so much greater than the fear that comes from being in a toxic relationship, being subjected to physical or emotional abuse, and from being told daily that they are unworthy.

It is this feeling of loneliness that also gives you the inner desire to seek solitude and experience transcendental meditation, healing, yoga, and nutritional retreats. You want to create that inner peace, that safety, or that aloneness time at least for a brief, temporary period because doing so has the power to relieve you of the anguish you feel inside.

Of course, your preference would be to be surrounded by loving people who totally understand you, get you, and hear you, people with whom you can just be yourself. But the truth is that most people don't do this; they find it hard to make the choice with whom to spend their time, and they stay surrounded by people who have opposing values. They need to gain the clarity, the strength, and the wisdom I have shared so far for them to break free.

When you perceive that you don't have the ability to change your personal circumstances, you will yearn for a connection with another human being. In this absence, you seem to default to your old habits and are willing to do anything you can to find someone to argue with, hug, or physically touch.

Some of you may just have a warped perspective on life, but for many others, the extreme negativity of it all conjures such emotions, feelings and desires within in that moment in time. They most likely don't know or are aware of how much of it they might actually follow through with or repeat.

But I'm just conjecturing. From those moments when the pain, suffering, and torture of being alone become so intense, some people would be willing to subject themselves to anything just so that they don't have to continue alone.

This behavior also is present in people who are staying in marriages, relationships, or jobs with a knowing that comes from the deepest parts of themselves that they shouldn't be in that relationship. They inwardly know that they should have listened to the inner voice that knows and should have walked away from the unfulfilled relationship they had been in for a long time.

Let me share with you Paul's inspirational story on how personal and spiritual development helped him identify what caused his disharmony, pain, and loneliness, and how through addressing the behaviors, habits, and beliefs he had built over a lifetime, he was able to address his life problems at the root. It is at the seed level that he saw how easily it was to plant seeds that activate the switches that turn on his inner light. At that point, his path to a truly inspired life was well illuminated.

I met Paul at our common friend's book launch; we ended up chatting for at least an hour. At the end of the evening, he asked for my business card. He complimented me by saying that all we had discussed rang true to his heart; he told me he would love to book a consultation.

I recall how when we first met, he considered himself an extremely lucky person who had everything going for him—a supporting and loving family and an outgoing personality. Paul was humble and confident enough in equal measure to communicate with people from all occupations, and he felt that he had more mates than the famous footballer David Beckham!

Paul was in a long-term relationship, worked with some very inspiring people, and had traveled to many parts of the world. He described himself as someone who was driven to succeed and make the most of the very short time he had on this planet.

Since a very young age, Paul was unwilling to follow society's conveyor belt of life. He wanted to break free and follow his personal bliss. Coming from Kent, a county known as the Garden of England with beautiful scenery but also known for its bad spots, chavs (southern English young working class person who behaves in a brash or vulgar manner and wears ostentatious clothing and jewellery), and ruthless street culture, he learned to be tough from a very early age.

Paul had a lot to live up to. He did all he could to fit in and to be tough. He learned to talk rough in order to survive the bullying, and at times, he played dumb to avoid being ridiculed for being the clever one.

Often, the people in the environment he had been born into, grew up in, and spent most of his time in assumed that he had it all together. Everyone around him thought that he had an ideal life, that he was settled in every way, and that he had a relationship most people would have envied.

Paul often did what most of these people did without ever knowing the truth and getting under the skin of the person he used to admire; he learned to live the life they were living without ever asking himself the fundamental question, is this really the case and what I want?

Most of you tend to always look over to your neighbor's yard and consider the lives of people you love and admire; you think they have it all together. You think the grass is greener on the other side, happiness is in their lives, and love is in their relationships.

You perceive things to be better in other people's existences than in your personal live and in situations outside yourself without ever knowing why this is so. This is partly because you often fail to see, acknowledge, and appreciate fully what you actually have. This is partially because you don't really know what those other people have gone through or currently are going through.

You forget that you might be seeing their model of the world through your own perceptions, that you are relating to their struggles through what your values are, and that you often never really get to know the truth of who these people really are. You fail to discover what it is that deep down they long for.

Making assumptions is what leads you to become infatuated with their lives, to see them as amazing people, and to think they have everything you could possibly imagine. You think they are living dream lives while you are trying to figure out how to get there in the shortest time possible.

Many of us since early childhood were taught to take things at face value and accept them as a given without ever really knowing the truth of the words we heard, the values we were given, and the totality of others' journeys. It this programming that later in life becomes your vanity, envy, and an illusion of your own making.

This was also the case with Paul. As we continued our coaching journey together, he started to share that many people he had grown up with envied his freedom that he deep down knew he had worked very hard to create. They were jealous of his entrepreneurial lifestyle in which he ran his own diary, worked whatever hours he wanted to work, and took as many days off work as he wished while most of the people around him were stuck in nine-to-five, restrictive lives in their offices.

As his business took off, Paul started to drive a nicer car and wore more-expensive clothes, and his appetite to grow grew stronger and stronger. For most people, that would be an amazing achievement; however, to his surprise, he started to feel the loneliness born from the very success he started to bring into his life. As he focused more on growing not only his business but also his personal and spiritual growth, he instantly became an outcast in the eyes of the people he loved and spent most of his time with. He learned how even some of the closest people to him whom he deeply cared for started to feel alienated, intimidated, and jealous of the changes, growth, and success he was bringing into his life. Despite continuing to spend time with the people he cared for and loved, he started to feel alone in the big vision he so wanted to achieve.

Since making a commitment to become a success, investing in his personal development, and going through the necessary changes to build those foundations, he found himself more and more in the loneliness of the cave of solitude.

I recall our first conversations when he shared his feelings about the constant sacrifices he had to make to fit in the environments he was familiar with and was accustomed to living in and belonging to. This separation, this nagging feeling, and the necessity of making choices that detached him from his old reality was also what at the beginning of our journey he feared most.

His entire being knew he had to change if he wanted to live an inspired life, but his feelings also responded with a vengeance and a knowing that the more he started to grow mentally, emotionally, spiritually, and financially, the lonelier he felt. This was all in spite of the fact that he knew all the changes he was making were essential for the greater good he dreamed about and desired to create.

On a physical level, he had experienced loneliness in many areas of his life. As an entrepreneur, he spent a lot of time working from home, and that had taken him out of the regular social environment he once enjoyed. The banter and camaraderie was now minimal, and that made him feel withdrawn, isolated, and distant from the rest of the world.

Yet it was on a deeper level that he had the greatest problem in his mind. He knew that being an empowered, inspired entrepreneur with a big vision had already made him an outcast among so many of his social circuit and society itself. He also felt that having a global vision to serve humanity and act in a loving and compassionate manner toward the people of the world led only to pointing out the disparity between himself and the people he felt were disempowered, selfish, and out of touch with their inner feelings.

This is certainly what he used to perceive and would notice in other people before we started to dig deeper to find the seed of his discords. His journey led him to unearth lifetime façades he had built up so he could become clear on his values, broaden his vision, and learn about the importance of universal laws such as the law of balance, cause and effect, and the duality of our nature. The more he understood how he was infringing on other people's free will, freedom of choice, and ways of being, the more he understood the signals he was emitting that attracted the reality he was seeing.

As he started to embody the mindful principles of the TJS Evolutionary Method in his day-to-day living, Paul started to have clarity of thought, vision, and mission of what he truly wanted to do in this world.

The wisdom and the tools shared in each of our sessions helped him cope better with people and situations on a daily basis. Paul started to exponentially raise his conscious awareness and consider greater things he could achieve. Starting on an inner journey, addressing the voices within, and opening a dialogue with his critical inner child helped him really see the hidden truths about himself from a new perspective. He saw with clarity how the way he had been living his life would not give him the results he was seeking. He acknowledged with certainty how his actions, behaviors, and beliefs had resulted from the way he had grown up and had had a great effect on the way he felt about himself and others.

In time, Paul became better at observing, learning, and listening to what the people he came into contact with were truly communicating to him, what their motives were, and what they wanted from him.

I kept inviting him to social events, various seminars, and workshops so he could practice what he had learned in every session and determine what else he might need my help with. Each time he came to those events I saw how easy it became for him to see beyond what everyone else in the room could see.

As he developed the ability to see through his own life obstacles, he learned how to observe other people's issues without getting involved in them or being drawn or pulled into other people's agendas by their forceful energy. That was something that in his past had happened to him frequently and make him deal with other people's needs and wants.

This expansion of the awareness of his inner being helped him see the positives and negatives of his ways of feeling, thinking, and being as well as those of others. The shift from an old paradigm to a new way of thinking created the strength he required to distance himself from those who drained his energy, ridiculed him, and mocked him about his global vision and mission.

He learned that sometimes in life, to pursue his dreams and live an inspired life, he would have to make choices that would disconnect him from the people he had grown up with, dated, worked with, and shared many great memories with. As he finally made the decision to walk away from a disempowered relationship, he suddenly had more energy, enthusiasm, and time to pursue the outcomes he truly wanted to achieve.

For him, loneliness wasn't necessarily about being alone in a physical sense. It had an awful lot to do with being alone in his heart and in his relationship and being disconnected from his spirit.

During one of our sessions together he shared how being of greater service, wanting to change the world, and becoming successful made him feel extremely lonely. No matter who might have helped him along the way, he occasionally found himself in the cave of wretched solitude and wondering why that was.

Having gone through these experiences, Paul acknowledged that he had learned a great deal about himself along the way. He recognized how being lonely was not a nice feeling for him. He learned how sometimes this lonely feeling made him doubt himself and others, and that created only more separation and distrust. He understood that the notion of being all alone in the mission and vision he had created for himself also made him put his dreams to one side and be distracted by people and activities that didn't support his highest values.

He came to understand how important it was to invest in his spiritual growth to help him navigate his emotional outbursts by using his body's alarms and the eight façades to help him deal with life's adversity.

Through this personal development, Paul laid the solid foundations required for the big vision he is now focusing on and is inspired to build. He came to acknowledge the importance of moving away from worrying about short-term gains and avoid the long-term pain that most entrepreneurs experience at the beginning of their entrepreneurial journeys.

All the insights along this journey led him to surrender to the intelligence within, to the same intelligence you and everyone around you has that is well hidden from your conscious awareness and is now awakening as you read this book.

This divine intelligence given to you at birth knows that you are part of a whole, and are powerful and eternal. By awakening this intelligence in you, you learn to build the trustworthy connections you need to live in wholeness. Trusting this intelligence within, just like Paul, you too can become the explorer of your own galaxy.

He learned how the unity, the connection to the spirit, and common ground that most people seek yet can't seem to find to become creators was an essential component for building the foundations of trustworthy relationship with self and others. This newfound trust got him to stop doubting himself about the greater good he was trying to make that often left him wondering what the point of it all was. We explored further his lifestyle choices and daily habits and looked from a physical point of view how he lived his daily life. He recognized how dedicating his time to starting a business at times led him to completely neglect his social life and make excuses to avoid being in contact with others.

Paul spent a lot of time going back over his pain, and each time we had a session, he started to get clear on the seeds that led him to his pain. He also spent a lot of time and energy reflecting on what things he did that grew into the happiest moments in his life. He felt that they happened when he was experiencing new things with a group of friends who shared common values and each other's company and had a zest for life, adventure, and fun.

Sometimes, he would come to me feeling as though he had thrown himself into work in order to buy that lifestyle again. He thought that perhaps his drive to be successful financially made him believe that he could buy his happiness. He thought money would bring him the power to buy what he desired and the wholeness he deep down yearned for. He thought that having a lot of money, being successful, and proving to himself that he had made it would be the answer to his lonely heart and all his problems.

Paul learned the experiences he was having not only exacerbated his problems but also were at the root of his loneliness, the darkness within, and the daily fears that paralyzed his being.

As Paul grew stronger, more confident, and rich in spiritual wisdom, he confessed to me how lonely he had been in his whole life one way or another. From a very young age, he always knew he was different from others. While many kids he grew up with made as many derogatory comments about as many people as possible, he never felt good about being part of that or in their presence when they would behave in such an unloving way toward others who were different from the norm.

It just didn't feel right to him; he could never understand why, and he felt that maybe he was dumb to some degree, that he was not good enough, that he was below other people for not being able to fit in with these people he spent most of his childhood with.

Paul kept refocusing within to find the solutions to his daily problems and tackled every life obstacle that prevented him from living the life he always wanted and knew he deserved to have. One of the major shifts that helped him liberate his soul was accepting that he was not responsible for other people's misfortunes and feelings, that each soul exercises its own free will and freedom of choice and goes through different stages of spiritual growth.

He acknowledged within himself that each person evolves at a different rate, and he was simply more a wandering spirit who had chosen to grow faster than most people around him. This created a great sense of relief; he stopped comparing himself with others, let go the need to passively control other people's choices that challenged his values, and listen to his true voice.

The more he let go the need to control others, their opinion of him, and his opinion of himself, the more he started to feel an inner harmony. The freer he felt, the more confident he became in his abilities, skills, and capability to make a difference and play his part in changing the world.

This journey from the wretched cave of solitude led him to switch on his internal light that shined his path toward the life oasis of inspired living that he now enjoys along with the benefits it brings. He learned how to control the switch that turned on the flow of the love energy as well as the one that triggered and invoked various lopsided emotions including rejection, judgment, and being lonely.

As he furthered his knowledge about ways to quickly switch off the noises in his head, he started to fine-tune his internal receiver, to listen with clarity to his authentic voice and the wisdom within, and to access and honor the knowing of his heart. His confidence increased, he freed himself from the lifelong, limiting beliefs he had had about himself, and he brought himself closer to his dream.

Paul created new empowering beliefs, habits, and behaviors he required to achieve all that he wanted to create in his life. Paul's energy shifted; each time I saw him, he was more and more being his authentic self.

Although at times he still feels being a successful entrepreneur is a lonely place to be, he now enjoys his alone time and accepts it as part of strengthening his inner resilience, listening to his soul's voice, and expanding his horizons. Paul's monthly discipline helped him continue to grow spiritually, mentally, and emotionally as his awareness about the magic that life can be expanded exponentially.

After each session, Paul leaves having overcome one more challenge, with a new insight, and with certainty that each challenge that life presents him is there to help him transcend to the next level.

He saw how the TJS Evolutionary Method helped him master the science of balancing his perceptions and seeing adversity through the eyes of gratitude. Paul now enjoys being in the flow of the rhythm of life and feeling inspired and creative; he is eager to quench his thirst for more spiritual knowledge. This awakening from living life on snooze is what every soul seeks on its spiritual path. It is through this journey that he also got inspired to write his first book *Bulletproof Entrepreneur* to help entrepreneurs realize that their greatest wealth is their health. How by staying fit and healthy while running their business they could achieve great business success.

Let the experiences, the insights, and the wisdom shared in this book be the lasting reminder, light, and inspiration you need to help you transmute your apparent loneliness into wholeness. Remember who you really are, the result of intelligent design who has infinite abilities to destroy and create life. You are a product of love and light that when activated it can illuminate darkness.

The lessons that Paul, others, and I have taken from various life adversities are there as guiding tools to help you come to your own conclusions about how the loneliness and life adversities you experience switch off your light and disconnect you from the source energy that love is.

Once you acknowledge the issues that create your apparent loneliness, you are then in a position to do something about it. Choose to change your personal circumstances and walk the path that leads from the cave of wretched solitude and into the oasis of inspired living.

From this resourceful state, you can then always remain the light without having the need to control who sits in its presence, who needs to see it, who needs to come to it, or at what intensity it needs to shine. Your job is to give yourself permission to shine, to keep cleaning, and to keep polishing your own mirror.

You are here to create your life, live purposefully, and to uncover your magnificent life purpose. Be the choice that makes an extraordinary difference in the world and leaves behind an immortal legacy that serves the evolution of humanity.

You exist because you are love, you are the answer to world peace, and you have the ability to listen to your soul's call for love. That call has been there before you, is there now from you to you, and will be there in your future and your children's future. Embody love in every inch of your being; in doing so, you will transmute your deceptive loneliness into beautiful wholeness. Learn to illuminate your heart and see how easily it is for you to become the light beacon that other souls can use to find their way back home, back to their inner light, back to the source energy that created us all—love.

Thank you for coming on this journey with me. I trust all you have read has inspired your wondrous soul, opened your heart, and equilibrated your mind. All that I have shared has equipped you with the knowledge, tools, and wisdom you will require to dismantle the illusions of your lower mind, switch on the light that illuminates your higher mind and remain centered in your heart.

—Tony J. Selimi

A peaceful mind is priceless,
a loving heart is timeless!

CHAPTER 12

WHAT NEXT?

After reading this book, you might feel inspired to read *A Path to Wisdom* and *A Path to Excellence* and learn how to use the TJS Evolutionary Method: the ALARM and the eight façades to unleash your genius. The more façades you unveil, the more you unveil your inner light. The deeper you dig, the faster you will find your inner diamond.

To take this work to the next level, I would recommend you learn both methods and apply them across all eight key areas of your life. As you apply them to your life, you will access parts of you that may be currently asleep or that you may be unaware of, but they are there to help you pave your way to living a meaningful, purposeful, and inspiring life.

Learning both methods will balance your perceptions, open your heart, and help you maximize your prime asset, yourself. The alarm and each of the eight façades are there as a guide to help you navigate the journey to magnificence, wholeness, and living a prosperous life.

Daily applying the two methods will help you create balance, live a healthy life, and find inner peace. You can use them to create, build, and maintain trustworthy, transparent, and authentic connections. As you learn to apply them daily, you will become inspired to do more, be more, and love more.

I would be honored to learn about you as you have taken the time to learn about me. I love nothing more than being of service to you and to the evolution of human consciousness, and I want to help you unleash the infinite wisdom of your being.

It gives me tremendous joy to assist global leaders, entrepreneurs, corporations, and people from all occupations to unlock the mountain of value that you may be sitting on to make a global difference. A balanced mind and an illuminated heart will help you harness your infinite abilities to innovate, transform, and utilize your creativity for the good of all.

Focusing on what you love and what inspires you creates a purpose and nurtures your creative genius. Enjoy your life not just for the destination but also for the triumphs and the mistakes you will find along your path; they are major parts of your growth.

Reaching a state within you that is peaceful, loving, and balanced will help you appreciate living in gratitude, acceptance, and certainty. From this state of awareness and being, inspiration will come to you naturally when least expected. Any expression of your being that goes to others can touch their hearts only when it comes from your inner truth.

You may also choose to book me to speak at your events, attend any of my events, talks, seminars, and workshops. Come to any of my retreats, download my online training programs, or work with me privately. To see what's coming up or to get in touch with me, please visit www.tonyselimi. com and don't forget to sign up to receive my free newsletter packed with inspirational articles, tools, and special offers.

Finally, if you love to inspire, contribute, and be of service, please review this book and help me reach and inspire people at every corner of our planet and from all walks of life. I love to reward you for taking the time to do so.

Here's how you can help my mission.

1. Write a review of this book and share it with the world.
2. Post it on Amazon, iTunes, on your website, blog, Facebook, LinkedIn, Twitter, Instagram, or another publication.

    Tweet about it @TonyJSelimi, and send a link or a screenshot to reviews@tonyselimi.com.

3. Receive a link to download a free MP3 meditation to help you center your being.

4. Automatically be entered in a drawing to win various prizes available to you only as a reviewer of the book.

If you have any tips on how to overcome loneliness or be more connected socially, mentally, emotionally, and spiritually, please do share them in my social media profiles!

Last, your challenge now is to embody all you have learned, apply it daily, and make the choice to let love be your first choice in all that you do, feel, and think. Daily choose to live in greatness, grace, and gratitude.

Good luck!

ACKNOWLEDGMENTS

A book is always a collection of the thoughts, experiences, and knowledge of many individuals. It would have been impossible for me to write this book without the forty-five years of contributions by thousands of people who have been part of my life since the day I was born. I gained the wisdom I shared in this book by fusing my academic background, a library of scientific literature, and popular personal and spiritual development books I have read. It came from amazing blogs, workshops I have held and attended, and the many chats and interviews I have had with clients, family members, friends, and people from everywhere.

Let me start by saying thank you to my mum, Lutvije Selimi, for her strength, patience, and unconditional love. Without all the support and challenges she gave me, I would not be the person I am today. She taught me the life skills that helped me survive adversity, great values that paved the way to my becoming who I am today, and the importance of speaking my truth. Your extraordinary life journey has been a great inspiration for me throughout my life and in writing this book. I love you.

The loneliness you and I have endured, especially since the morning of November 25, 2006, when Dad passed away, and the many life-changing events that followed has been a paramount factor in my writing this book.

Just like you, billions of people globally are lonely. They sacrifice their own lives to make sure their children have a better chance for better lives, and in old age, most of them remain alone.

I know I have not been there with you as much as we both would have loved. I trust, love, appreciate and have gratitude to you for all the sacrifices and the love you have given me that is captured in this life manual. I wrote this book to help people overcome their apparent loneliness, listen to their hearts' calling, and connect with one another in a more meaningful way.

This book is my way of honoring you, my Dad Shaqir Selimi, and everyone in my life. It is my way of expressing my appreciation for every life adversity that led me to feeling rejected, abandoned, and fearful as well as for the many wonderful people who helped me on this illuminous journey to balance my lopsided perception of loneliness and open my heart to love and gratitude.

A special thanks to my sister Feleknaz and her husband, Xhavit; my sister Hanumsha and her husband, Besir; my sister Selime; my sister Drita and her husband, Aziz; my brother, Selim, and his wife, Flora; my nieces, Reziana, Adelina, Valdeta, Bernadeta, Besa, Deliza, Arjeta; my nephews, Ardian, Berat, Rinim, Elzan, Arijan; and the rest of my family for their support and challenge, unfailing love, and, in my absence, for looking after Mum. I love you and thank you with every beat of my heart.

Thank you to the many people who have been part of my journey, all the teachers, healers, coaches, professors, work colleagues, friends, and spirit guides. To Joel Van der Molen, Timea Van der Molen, Phil Carvil, Hans Schumann, Michele Scataglini, Michael Bell, Paul N Miller, Shelley J Whitehead, Benjamin Morley, Daniel and his father Andrew Priestley, Darshana Ubl, Mindy Gibbins-Klein, Nora Rodriguez, Robert Bricout, Sarbjit Hear, Zuzana Solteszova, Tuna Sejdi, Tuna Sejdi, Adam Frewer, Laurie Cagno, Mike Markovski, Paul McMonagle, Sue Bannister, and many other clients for all their support and the knowledge they shared and for letting me play a role in the movie of their lonely and likewise inspiring lives.

I have been blessed to be loved and equally be challenged by extraordinary people. A big thank you to Dr. John Demartini for his time, unconditional love, and inspired teachings that helped me illuminate my mind. Your magic, teachings, and determination have been paramount factors in my quest for life's truths. During the Breakthrough and the Prophecy Experiences, I learned so much about the healing power of unconditional love. I faced my lies, illusions, and fears and inspired myself to expand my vision. I learned the importance of perusing universal truths and why honoring my highest values helps me acquire the highest rewards. I thank you and love you from the essence of my being.

To Todor Stamenov, Mouna Salih, Stuart Hall, Marcello Gregorovic, Amir Wender, Anna Orchard, Stephen Jones, Nick Frank, and Stephen Morallee, who see me at my very best and my very worst. Thank you for your time, your love, your nurturing, laughs, dancing, and for your ever-present love and unwavering support. Thank you for your patience and for helping me keep my promise to be at my best always! Your love and words of encouragement always come at just the right time and in ways that are more meaningful to me than you can imagine!

Thank you to all the amazing authors whose books I have read, scientists, the miracles of John of God in Brazil, and Sr. M. Callisita, MC, at the Mother Teresa Center for giving me their written permission to use her quote. To the founders of the International Academy of Consciousness, to Wagner Alegretti, Nanci Trivellato, Rodrigo Montenegro and all the teachers there for their ongoing love, support, and teachings.

I thank you, the reader, for purchasing this book, for sharing your experience with the world, and for all the gifts you bring into this world.

Once in a while, a special soul or a guardian angel will come into your life. Anthony Wade, known as Dr. Voice, is a kindred spirit that came into my life, touched my heart, and nurtured my wondrous and wounded soul with his presence and love. Most of all it is through his amazing presentations and vocal training that I learned to reconnect with my true, authentic voice. I love you and thank you for every moment we share, for your friendship, presence, and time, and for being a source of immense wisdom, love, and light.

To all the readers of my best-selling book *A Path to Wisdom* who took the time to write to me, share their breakthroughs, and wrote online reviews. To Dr. Josephine Ojiambo, Jack Wade, Matt Wade, Simone Vincenzi, Jellmaz Dervishi, Lia Raw, Annik Rau, Andrew Gray, Martha Friedlander, Jasmina Preshova, Mirela Sula, Melvin Carlile, Sara Troy, Dianna Boner, Marija Stamenova, Daniel Meekins, and many other special people from all over the world who have supported me in this journey to bring and share the message of love, healing, truth, equality, and heart-centered way of living and leading. To all the people from around the world for sharing their breakthroughs and miracles that manifested in their lives after downloading TJS Meditation Solutions and consistently meditated for 90 days.

This book wouldn't have been possible without my reviewers, Patryk Wezowski, Antony Welfare, Dawattie Basdeo, Jenny Garrett, Harun Rabbani, Melanie Le Roux, Klementyna de Sternberg Stojalowska, Rami Baz, Jo Hetherington, Daniel Browne, Katharine Wolf, Ayman Najafi, Sandra Wick, Baybars Altuntas, Shay Allie, Elaine Kennedy, and Dr. Kim Jobst.

To Vicki Wusche, Farhan Rehman, Marcus Stone, Rodney Van der Molen: your dedication to help me improve and clean up the grammar was nothing short of astonishing. I love you and thank you for being a light that has kept my path shining bright, for being caring, and for being thoughtful.

Finally, to Tina Colbert, Elisabeth D, Peter Le, and Martin M from Balboa Press the self-publishing division of Hay House, and the entire team of experts for their expertise and support needed to transform my manuscript and turn it into a beautiful book distributed to billions globally.

Thank you to everyone who has supported me with my dedication to my life's work. I am honored by your trust and am in awe of your vision for a better world. Through your presence, I have learned to become a better listener, and that has allowed me to yield the knowledge and the wisdom I now share with you and the whole world.

Thanks are also due to many people for offering their own stories and recollections and providing expert commentary and insights. Most of the people mentioned throughout my book have wholeheartedly shared their personal stories and have given me their permission to use their names. There are few people whose names I have deliberately changed or withheld to safeguard their privacy. Please accept my gratitude anonymously.

Finally, this book wouldn't have been possible without the many long hours, sleepless nights, and the sacrifices, commitment, consistency, and the discipline required for my soul and me to work in synchronicity to bring this book to fruition. Thank you, and I love you.

ABOUT THE AUTHOR

A former teenage soldier, a homeless person on the streets of London, and then a best-selling author, Tony J. Selimi is a professional speaker, author, coach, and business consultant. His clients include celebrities, MPs, doctors, scientists, therapists, coaches, healers, PTs, entrepreneurs, leaders, senior executives of companies such as Microsoft, SAP, Bank of America, Ignis Asset Management, Deutsche Bank, Ernst & Young, Santander, Vandercom, and Mishcon de Reya across EMEA, Asia and the United States.

Tony is a thought leader, inspired visionary, entrepreneur, and ambassador for the evolution of human consciousness. Globally, Tony provides answers to questions and practical solutions to life's challenges in talks, workshops, one-on-one coaching, mastermind groups, retreats, articles, and radio and TV interviews as well as through his books and online downloads of his TJS Evolutionary Meditation Solutions.

Tony is a rare and a gifted man whose span of experience and study encompasses a broad scope of knowledge. Originally trained as an electrical and electronic engineer, he has now developed his integrated approach to coaching, healing of physical and emotional pain, and unlocking people's true potential. Using his TJS Evolutionary Method: the ALARM and the eight façades, he takes people on a deep, inner journey to tap into their inner wisdom, recognize their abilities, and use their knowledge to make faster and better decisions and choices that are aligned with their highest values. He also uses his method to bring about purpose and value led transformations to his corporate clients.

He is a human behavior and cognition expert, an educator who loves teaching and passing on all he has learned to those who are called to be more, to think more, to contribute more, and to love more so they can unleash and maximize their human potential.

Prior to Tony becoming the See-Through Coach, also known fondly as Dr. Love, he worked in senior, high-pressure IT roles in a wide range of sectors including transport, retail, government, and recruitment. Parallel to his personal and spiritual development, he spent fifteen years working, learning, and building a very successful business career; he won awards, and effectively led, managed, and delivering large-scale, multimillion-pound IT programs.

The experience of working in the corporate world, overcoming many personal and professional challenges, and coaching many people gave Tony a unique insight on the pressures, the challenges, and the magnitude of issues his clients face daily.

Tony is the number-one, international, best-selling author of *A Path to Wisdom: How to Live a Healthy, Balanced, and Peaceful Life*. His book was short-listed for many awards including Management Book of the Year and is endorsed by many of the world's renowned public figures including the human behavior specialist Dr. John Demartini.

Tony is a University College London (UCL) engineering graduate who studied many life disciplines and received a number of awards. He is a qualified coach recognized by a number of reputable institutions including the International Coaching Federation, the Institution of Leadership and Management, Demartini Institute, the Complementary Therapists Association, and Martin Brofman's Foundation of Advanced Healers. He is a certified Reiki master teacher.

Tony is no stranger to the media, having appeared in various national magazines including *Soul and Spirit*, *Global Women*, *Migrant Women*, *Accelerate Your Business*, Changing *Careers Magazine*, *Consciousness Magazine*, *Your Wellness*, *Time Out*, and *Soul Mate Relationship World Summit*, and TV and radio shows including Voice of America, Gaydio, and Spirit Radio.

He gives inspirational talks on a range of topics including leadership, entrepreneurship, the evolution of consciousness, peace, well-being, spirituality, healing, energy, and vibration. Tony has been a keynote speaker at the Animas

Coaching Institute, Raw Fest, Love Spirit Festival, Be Inspired, Conscious Leadership events, private functions, and Mind Body Spirit festivals. He hosts regular webinars with his clients entitled Conversations with Your Heart.

Like a transparent mirror, Tony is known for his ability to see through people's problems, behaviors, thought patterns, and disempowering beliefs and help them rid themselves of lies that conceal their inner truth. He helps people speak their truth, find answers and solutions to life's obstacles, clarify their values, and cope better with their daily pressures, demands, and life's obstacles. He helps many get to the cause of their issues, clarify and expand their lives' vision and mission, and unleash their interstellar existence.

Tony helps people increase their productivity and longevity, balance their perceptions, and master their emotions so they can purposely and positively move forward. He assists men and women in becoming balanced, valued, and heart-centered leaders.

Tony is paving the way for soulful and heart-centered leadership to become a part of our day-to-day life and in every company. He loves to inspire people globally to heal their body-mind, expand, grow, connect, communicate, and love.

Tony is a world ambassador of peace, love, and gender and sexuality equality. He advocates mindfulness, personal development, and coaching as an empowering choice through which businesses, educational systems, governments, leaders, adults, and children can unlock their true potential.

He shares his message of the importance that coaching, mindfulness, and meditation has on personal and professional life and in our communities, society, and universally.

Tony loves to speak, teach, and inspire people globally to realize the love and the wisdom that lives in each human being. His words of wisdom inspire minds, open hearts, and encourage people to live meaningful and inspired lives.

He is known for creating amazing, lasting, life-long transformations in people and in organizations. Tony's philosophy and revolutionary understanding of the power of love are changing the lives of millions of people all over the world. His clients experience a sense of relief and increased energy, performance, and focus. They feel inspired, peaceful, grounded, and connected to their infinite wisdom of love.

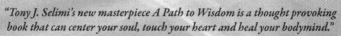

"*Tony J. Selimi's new masterpiece A Path to Wisdom is a thought provoking book that can center your soul, touch your heart and heal your bodymind.*"

Dr John Demartini, International best-selling author of The Values Factor

A PATH TO WISDOM

How to live a **balanced**, **healthy** and **peaceful** life

USA BEST BOOK
AWARDS
FINALIST
USABookNews.com

TONY JETON SELIMI

A PATH TO WISDOM

Distractions prevent us from listening to the inbuilt alarm our bodies use to alert us when something is wrong. Ignoring our inner wisdom is the cause of disease, aging, and psychological disorders. Unless attended, life adversities have the power to bring us out of our natural state of healthy balance and into lower-mind, animal behaviors that prevent us from realizing our highest expressions of ourselves.

Judgment and rejection are two of the biggest killers on the planet, especially judgment and rejection of ourselves. Based on my life experiences, I often asked my inner being what would be possible if we could get out of judgment, rejection, and perceptions of our lower-mind selves and go into the divine nature of our higher mind and see with clarity how every human trait is there to bring us back to equilibrium in our hearts.

This book is for you if you are ready to go on a deeper exploration of self to unravel parts of you that you don't love or that you reject, and if you are in pain that you may not currently be aware of. It includes exercises to help you identify the disempowered parts of yourself, break through your fears, and overcome obstacles that prevent you from living a balanced, healthy, and peaceful life.

You will learn how to use the TJS Evolutionary Method: the ALARM to create balance in all of the eight key areas of life: Business, Career, Finances, Mental, Emotional, Physical, Relationship, and Love. It is through each pillar of this method that you acknowledge, listen, act, and respond to your authentic voice that is there to guide you to take back the reins of your life and to harness the healing power of love, speaking your truth, and honoring your highest values. Doing all the exercises with a childlike curiosity will help you to use your innate, intelligent, built-in alarm to deepen your understanding of yourself, awaken you to your true calling, and honor your spirit, greatness, and wisdom. You can use this method in your business to bring mindfulness to your employees, implement value lead transformations, and improve business processes, sales, and customer interactions.

This proven method was developed over thirty years of heartfelt research and amassed, phenomenal knowledge; it is a way to establish an easy path to healing. The alarm consists of five pillars: acknowledge, love, achieve, results, and miracles, all of which help you create balance, inner peace, and great health. Use this method and complete the exercises in the book to learn how to

- acknowledge and own your power (be assertive, influential, and in control);

- listen to your body's wisdom to harness the infinite wisdom of love (heal your body and mind and honor your soul);

- accept your authentic, true self and achieve higher states of awareness and intelligence (activate you higher mind, become certain, and be true to who you really are);

- reconnect to your life's purpose with greater clarity and focus and bring about the results you dream about (live meaningfully and generate the results you desire); and

- master your life, live your dreams, and manifest miracles (give infinite value, receive wealth, and live a miraculous life).

Learning and applying the TJS Evolutionary Method: the ALARM will inspire you to be more, think more, create more, contribute more, and love more. The more you listen within, the faster you can create the shifts you desire in your outer reality.

Read this book cover to cover to silence your mind, create inner peace, and activate your built-in healing powers. The more you embody the wisdom written in every word, paragraph and page, the more you start to center your being, awaken your genius, and inspire the Leader in you. For more information please go to: www.apathtowisdom.com

BIBLIOGRAPHY

Cacioppo, J. &. (2008). *Loneliness: Human nature and the need for social connection*. New York.: W.W. Norton & Company, Inc: New York.

Cellan-Jones, R. (2014, December 2). *Stephen Hawking warns artificial intelligence could end mankind*. Retrieved from BBC UK Technology News: http://www.bbc.co.uk/news/technology-30290540

http://psychology.about.com/od/psychotherapy/a/loneliness-can-be-contagious.htm. (n.d.). Loneliness-can-be-contagious.

http://www.motherteresa.org/layout.html. (n.d.).

http://www.newrepublic.com/article/113176/science-loneliness-how-isolation-can-kill-you. (n.d.).

http://www.nytimes.com/2008/12/08/opinion/08cohen.html?_r=0. (n.d.).

http://www.psmag.com/books-and-culture/nick-bostrom-superintelligence-singularity-technology-future-books-90067. (n.d.).

Shulevitz, J. (n.d.). *The Lethality of Loneliness*. Retrieved from New Republic: http://www.newrepublic.com/article/113176/science-loneliness-how-isolation-can-kill-you

Wikiquote. (n.d.). *Wikiquote*. Retrieved from https://en.wikiquote.org/wiki/Nikola_Tesla

Notes

Notes

Notes

Notes

Printed in the United States
By Bookmasters